SERVING FOR A LIVING

BY

JAY KAY

A Servers Guide for Making Money

CREDITS

I would like wish a special thanks to;

Scott Supplee
For the cover design
scott@supleedesigns.com

Dave O'Sullivan
Author, Editor, and Screenplay Writer
Osullivan.dave34@gmail.com

My fellow coworkers who put up with me everyday

And the thousands of guests who made this book possible

Copyright 2012

Forward

Several years back I wrote a booklet entitled "The Customers Guide To Breakfast and Lunch" which, was written out of frustration (and to make a few bucks) with my job. I would find myself after each shift in the alley of the restaurant or at a bar, drinking, smoking and bitching about the day's events. I finally decided to put pen to paper and the rest is history.

What Jay has done here is taken it to a whole new level or, stratosphere and has given you a back stage pass to the circus of the service industry. Serving for a Living is not only a great read, it is a must read for patrons and insiders. It's funny and brutally honest; it's absurd and even unbelievable for those who have never worked in "The Business". I worked with Jay and we served in the trenches together and had some pretty hairy days as well as fun ones. He nailed it with this work and exposes the under belly of the trade. Serving for a Living is just that, serving the public.

Unless you have worked at a restaurant you can't imagine what it is like and how you are treated. It's being in the face of the public and dealing with the worst humanity has to offer, and, sometimes, the best. People think that serving is easy, menial and a low rung on the social ladder. You have to smile as you eat a shit sandwich and say "man that's good!" Jay has taken his brilliant blog and turned it into a book that will change the way you look at the "lowly server".

Having spent twenty years in the business myself I found this book to be a guide or bible if you will, for servers just starting out and patrons who can now have a clue. From the blatantly rude to the socially retarded to the complete pleasure to serve you customer, Jay captures them all and holds up a mirror. Everyone can learn something from this. Serving can be a thankless, stressful choice for a job but if you're lucky, you can actually you can meet some great people and make some good money. Restaurant work is sex, drugs and rock and roll (sans the music) and it's all in here, from work place sex to drug and alcohol use, this book will have you up all night, just don't be late for your shift!

Dave O'Sullivan

TABLE OF CONTENTS

1. Introduction
2. Types of Guests
3. Groups
4. Regular Customers
5. Favorites
6. Difficult Guests
7. Tipping
8. Complaints
9. Frugal
10. Staffing
11. Service
12. Workaholic
13. Catering
14. Management
15. Philosophies
16. Profit
17. How to Make Money
18. Occupations
19. Miscellaneous
20. My Experiences Out
21. Holidays
22. Summary

I

Introduction

This is account of what goes on every day across the world and what goes through a servers mind all day long. This book is comprised of a series of true accounts extracted from my blog of the same name. I am older and henceforth a little cranky and less tolerable. Some, if not all of my material comes off as sarcastic, aloof, and hopefully entertaining.

There are a lot of reasons I do this but the most prominent one is I can't do anything else. In 1973 I got a job as a server and loved it. I worked part time in a hotel, worked 35 hours a week and made $400 A WEEK. Not bad money for a full time college student, studying Hotel, Food, Service Management. 38 years later, I'm doing it again. Two reasons cause me to do this. One is the money is still good and I still love it!

I starting waiting tables when I was 18 at a steak house that I starting washing dishes for when I was sixteen. Gas was 33 cents a gallon back then. I always realized there was a lot of money to be made doing this without putting in a lot of hours. It is a great skill to possess because throughout my colorful career it has come in handy everywhere I have worked. I obtained a Hospitality degree in 1976 and my career eventually went to the executive management level with a major hotel chain. I worked my way up the ladder stopping at every occupation there is in the Food and Beverage world. From dishwasher to Food and Beverage Director, I have loved every minute of it. In the last 38 years I have done lots of things from Executive Committee management in a major hotel company, Sole Proprietor, Operations Director, Food and Beverage Director, Assistant General Manager, Executive Chef, ground breaking computer whiz, and a whole bunch of other stuff, we will not discuss in this book. The best position to experience is the "server' as there is no customer contact in this business as waiting on people every day.

Being too old to try to out-run the young whippersnappers of the industry, you know the guys who want to work 70 hours a week and do the six and seven day a week thing, I have semi-retired. I wait tables because I love it and the people I meet every day. The money is still as good now, as it was then. Remember when our Dads told us "no matter what you do, be the best at it". I believe I am the best.

Every day I drag these old bones out of bed at 5:30am and go to work. I work in a breakfast, lunch, and dinner family owned restaurant. It has 117 seats of which 52 of those are outside. It doesn't really matter which restaurant you work in because they are all pretty much the same. There are differences but nothing worth mentioning. A chef friend once told me after traveling the country with this major hotel company as we both did for years that "nothing ever changes except the zip code". We both got transferred to Manhattan to open a 2000 room hotel after we had both been with the company for over 10 years. He was right. Nothing new has happened in this industry since the conception of 2-1 Happy Hour.

After working at this restaurant for years and keeping my mouth shut about my opinions, I decided to write a Blog to release my frustrations. I have opinions about fellow employees, management and yes customers. I decided to share my thoughts with people so they can better understand what we, as servers, do every day and what the good, the bad and the ugly is in our occupation. I have seen it all and probably done it all. When you have been around as long as I have, you have seen way too much theft, romance in the workplace, sexual harassment, bad employees and even worse managers. I have also seen a lot of good stuff too so I will share all of my thoughts in this book. It is however more fun to poke at the funnier stuff of which most is of the negative side. I told you I was sarcastic!

My blog of the same name is still current unless it took you a really long time to get to read this book and I have died of old age at the ripe old age of 93. So if you're following the timeline and the publishing date correctly, check it out.

It's my love and my passion. I've had my ups and downs, mostly downs, probably because of the hours required to climb the corporate ladder, but it's all been worth it, as the experience I have gained, over the years, has allowed me the wherewithal to write this book.

For those of you who do this and those who know people who do this and for those of you who eat out (all of you), I dedicate this book the best working partner I ever had. She knows who she is.

I hope you not only enjoy this book as much as I have enjoyed writing it. If you are serving for a living, I hope you can learn something from it. Enjoy!!

2
Types of Guests

I enjoy my job because I encounter all different kinds of people every day. There is a reason to write about them as they all have unique qualities that make them noteworthy. I will now share with you some of my favorite types of customers.

I call him the Mayor because he knows 40% of the patrons, the owner and his Mom and most of the servers. He and his wife stop at four tables on the way in. He says hello to the owners shakes hands and has several visitors at his table throughout his stay. Now he orders. Two iced waters and a soup and half sandwich. That's right, that's all. The cup of soup is for his wife and the half sandwich is for him. $7.42 is the total bill and he has fulfilled his social requirement for the day. He will most likely get invited to a picnic or bar-b-que where he is required to bring a dish that he pick up at Publix on his way, instead of making potato salad at home. He will most likely bring his own bottled water and then drink someone else's beer. He leaves me $2 which is more than 20%. That's okay, except I could have used that four top, twice and for at least one meal per person. I don't bitch about this one because there is a lot of mileage to be gained. I stay close to this guy, as he knows people, which is great for job security and could be an ally if you ever need one. If someone he knows complains about me, not that it would ever happen; he will be in my corner and defuse the situation. I can continue to work, earn money and write about all this stuff so you can read it.

I have blogged before about people taking up space in the restaurant frequently but this one is a little different. A male customer comes in just after 12:30 and talks to the waitress and orders a coffee. As he sits in my section I fetch it for him. He snaps at me says he ordered Iced Coffee. I apologize and return with his Iced Coffee. I inquire if he is ready to order lunch and he just stares at me and replies, "I don't know, not now". I go back to the rest of my full station as it is lunch hour and I keep my eye on my man using the free Wi-Fi and taking up 4 seats in my area for the next two hours. I ask if he wants to order lunch as the kitchen closes in 15 minutes. He again snaps at me and tells me it's too late to order lunch. He now tells me he wants to talk to me **_outside_**. I explain that I am not going outside with him and anything he has to say he can say right here. He proceeds to tell me he is not leaving me a tip for two reasons.

First he is poor and second he claims the service was inadequate. I explain to him that it's no big deal if you don't leave me a tip. I can survive without the 40¢. I am not sure how I screwed up. He was drinking an Iced Coffee. We are not an internet café or Starbucks where coffee is the entrée or Yogurtology with free Wi-Fi. We are a full service restaurant with real food and real people, trying to make a real living. I am sorry that the man is poor and can't afford to take his medications, but that is not my problem. I have been asked to step outside before but, trust me, it wasn't over a cup of coffee.

It's getting a little ridiculous with the non-revenue producing meetings and office space, as 30% of my station camped today for over 2 hours. Monday there is a weekly meeting of ten with two meals, a few drinks for 2 hours. No one wants to sit next to them so they migrate to a section that was not mine. Today I had the return of a woman who was here last week for 5 hours. She ordered only one meal, consumed the space for four people for 5 hours. Listen up. A 20% tip doesn't cut it. Another couple having a meeting at another table in my section with a check for 2 coffees and a Blueberry muffin produced a $6.00 check, 3 hours. Another table with a Latté and a Coffee and no food on a 2 hour stay. Does the phrase "Get a Room" as in a meeting room mean anything to anyone today. I made $6.50 on the three tables in the time they spent there. 10 hours of occupied space and I think that I earned 65¢ an hour. Wow!

The 5 hour lady concerns me as she in impervious to the fact that she is using free Wi-Fi and my electricity, and preventing me from making any serious money. I am looking for a way to tell her she has outstayed her welcome without sounding like Bill Maher.

Next I would like to talk about couples. This subject has been explored by therapists, marriage counselors, and dating services. I offer no advice, just observation. I see couples who do not speak to each other during their entire visit. One reads a book while the other reads the paper; two actually both read the paper but never speak to each other. I wonder if they are happy and what things are like at home. I love communicating, so this confuses me. I also see couples where the man orders for the woman and vice versa. I don't understand as our menu is written in ENGLISH. We don't have an extensive wine list and the days of chivalry, in terms of ordering, are all but gone. Why does one party not let the other one speak? Does this go back to the days where women weren't allowed to speak, should be seen and not heard. Again I am no longer married and silence was never a part of my marriages. You'll just have to trust me on that one.

Again I offer no advice. I just do what I do and live with it. Once in a while when I look at the non-speaking party, I get a look from the ordering party that says "Hey, Hey Look at ME! I just thought it was weird.

Let me talk about the bar crowd. After working a regular breakfast shift 6:30am-2:30pm, I volunteered to work Amateur Bar Night. Volunteer is defined as working for no expected pay. The shift is 9:00pm to 3:00am, which is going to be followed by my regular breakfast shift tomorrow or later that day, depending how you look at it. What a crowd. Amateur bands from the local community come in to perform and their local following usually attends. After the $5.00 covercharge, some of these people, mostly college students are tapped out. The problem with people who don't have money is that they can't afford to drink or if they do, they cannot afford to tip. There is no charge for iced water, which becomes my biggest seller.

A total of four bands perform throughout the night, including set changes and about 1:30am my night is starting to wrap up. Now it's time to clean a cigarette butt laced patio area and move a bunch of 125 pound granite tables back into the restaurant to prepare for breakfast for the upcoming day. I do my paperwork and there is only $60 for my effort. I am tired now but nothing like what I will face tomorrow on 2 hours sleep.

Previous shifts like this have reeled in $100 to $200 per shift, not this time. Hey times are tough. I'm happy for the $60.

I think when we get older; we no longer enjoy large crowds of people, loud music, lyrics we can't understand and the late night hours. It is also requires some screwy hours. A split 16 hour shift, with 6 hours in between, is followed by an 8 hour shift on two hours of sleep the next day. No more Volunteering for this old man.

Let me go back to meetings. People who consume large amounts of space, small amounts of food, for extended periods of time, are considered "Squatters". Each seat in my station is worth about $2 every 45 minutes. We have the Governors, the Match.com people and a host of business people, who come in and take up space for hours on end. This really puts a damper on my "Turn and Burn" philosophy of making lots of money. Five people came in today and took up 8 seats for 2 hours and 15 minutes. I'll do the math for you that is $48. Spending $100 for breakfast or lunch and leaving me $20 doesn't work for me. 3 people ate and rendered one table of four useless for 1 ½ hours. I have couples come in, order two cups of coffee and two muffins, talk for hours, tie up four seats for over two hours and have an $8 check. They leave a $2 tip and assume I am happy.

Most people, I would say, have no idea that they are trying up valuable real estate or just don't care. We are a table service establishment and unlike Starbucks, you get your stuff, you pay and then nobody cares how long you stay or where you sit.

Don't people have offices anymore? I have a lanai, a backyard, a dining room and a living room that you can come over and sit in for hours if I think we are going to be HOURS and HOURS!

It doesn't seem fair to those people who want to eat and can't get a table, don't want to wait, and go somewhere else to eat. Let's not even mention the server, who is being punished financially because people are being inconsiderate. The coffee and muffin people should be good for, 3 turns, times 4 seats, times $2. That equals $24(not $2). Space is expensive and time is money. It takes a real diplomat to ask them to move on or to a smaller table, so exercise cautions my fellow servers.

Florida is the retiree capital of the United States. The economy and the people involved in their own finances have provided different fiscal scenarios for different people. You can tell who the retirees are. Most are regulars and they are not really on a schedule. Some care about the prices. Those are the ones who split entrees or just have pastries or desserts. Some don't care about money, representing the other segment, and they just want, what they want. You can tell the difference between the "well to do" and the "not so much". Different types of people make up my day, so it matters not to me what your financial situation is. Tipping here is not an issue as 20% of a $20.00 check is the same as a 10% tip on a $40.00 check.

Retirees are a huge part of my income. The tipping part doesn't concern me, but I question the variance between the "well to do" and the "not so much". When I retire, I would like to order what I want and not have to care about how much it cost.

The family experience is pretty predictable. There are lots of trips to the table, usually a huge mess on top and under the table and a lot of personalities to deal with. The parents, who for some reason don't want to cook special orders at home, decide to visit your restaurant. The kids, who are either unruly or, don't speak at all and the visitors. These visitors could be friends along for the free breakfast ride or the Grandparents who feel the need to be there. The parents usually order for the kids, pancakes, French toast, eggs, toast or muffins, and bagels. All of these things I am certain are not available in the home. The parents then order, no brainer, and the visitors order pretending the children are not there. Kids are great if you can talk to them, but that is not always the case. I am constantly looking for clues as to who to take instructions from. Don't try to get cutzie with the grandchildren and take the away the grandparents' time from a child. They may only see them once a year, and it's now. Check average is high and families usually tip well.

Try to figure out who is in charge and base your process on that information and what you have learned. Feed the kids first. Two reasons we do this is because it occupies the children and when the parents get their food they actually have time to eat. If you have kids you know what I mean. Remember children are children now, but they are future clients down the road.

People sit at the counter because they don't want to be left alone. These are people with a high level of social skills that prefer to interact with others. If they didn't want interaction, they would sit at a table by themselves so they could be left in peace. Almost all of the counter folks where I work are regulars. We know their names and their favorite things. We make them feel comfortable, that's our job. Two for dinner and the date thing is for nighttime and I work breakfast and lunch. They expect you to talk to them and provide speedy service. They are here to eat, chit chat, and run. We make that happen.

The single diner however wants to be left in peace. They do not want to chit chat, and usually have something to do, read, work or think. Recognize this when there is a "Table for one". Get the order, be efficient and stay away and you should be golden.

Remember to always put the check down right after the meal is put on the table so the guest can pay at their convenience, not yours. Remember they are usually on a tight time frame.

Identify your counter and single diners and act accordingly. We do have regular counter people who come in just to be with us. These folks are usually alone by choice, spouse is out of town, working, or it's their ritual. Talk to them when you have time and do your best to make them feel warm and fuzzy inside. Don't be afraid to introduce yourself to new people and almost all counter people are good tippers. I enjoy this part of my job.

Everyday people will get together over a meal to meet. It could be high finance, a deal, a proposal, a first date, friends or family who haven't seen each other for a while, but it will happen. Read it like a book so you know how to find your place in this meeting. Remember one thing; you are not part of the meeting. You may be ignored, not recognized for your purpose there, or asked to come back several times. Learn how to do this. If there is extensive conversation and the menus are still closed, get some beverages and introduce yourself and tell them you will be back when they are ready. Keep watching those menus. When you find the hole, go in, get what you need, and get out. Food down and check down and your job is done here. Don't interject on the first date and don't try to command the conversation, I'm sure you are not part of the deal. You can do all that stuff with your other folks that just come to eat, not meet.

Heads up and try to read everybody and everything in your station. Sometimes we are sent to tables to take orders and they are not ready. You know that because you know what's going on. The one who sent you may not. Go anyway and at least make a pass and look to make eye contact. If you know this table wants to wait, you can buy some time when you get busy. Sometimes it is as simple as a greeting, drink, and food order and done. Other times it is not. Always remember to be a true professional.

The other day two women come in with a two year old baby. Of course the baby was cute! As we all know babies enjoy playing with their food as much as they do eating it. Hey, they don't know any better. So we always expect a mess after the baby slips out of the restaurant for the well deserved nap. The clean up usually requires several towels or napkins, a broom and a dust pan and in extreme cases, a mop. This Mom was very apologetic during the entire meal and I reminded her that is was no problem. We get a lot of children and it is just part of life. However this time it was different. The Mom paid with a credit card and I processed the card and returned it to the table for signature. I then got stuck in the kitchen for a while. When I returned they were gone. To my surprise when I approached the table, not only was the table clean but Mom had even cleaned the floor. Wow!

I was impressed as most Moms don't clean up. They expect us to do it. Not only did she clean up, she left a 30% tip. Now that is the PERFECT MOM!

Researching over a vast period of time I have tried to find the differences between a meeting of the Boys and the Girls. The Boys usually show up early or on time as the Girls usually show up on time or late. Most Girls I have found usually get the meeting date wrong, something I rarely find in the Boys. The conversation is usually the same. It's usually about business, then sports, family and whatever. The women usually have a short or long gossip session, about who's doing what and to whom and the Boys do not. Waiting on them is easy as the meal is secondary to everything. Most of the Boys are matter of fact and complete their business and go back to work. The girls on the other hand seem not to be in a hurry to go anywhere. I have seen the Girls stay well past closing time which is something the Boys do not do. Traditionally the Boys have to go back to work where as the Girls don't seem to have a schedule. Tipping is not an issue here so I will not discuss it.

It's an exciting day as three generations of family arrive for breakfast. Grandma is a regular and she has brought the son, the daughter in-law and the two grandchildren in for a meal. This is an interesting scenario. First they order drinks, what the parents want to kids to drink. Then the bratty kids get their wish and we return with what the kids want to drink, first water and now chocolate milk and a hot chocolate. Pastries are ordered for starters, now extra napkins and extra plates. After four trips to the table, now we try to order breakfast. The parents order for the children, what the parents think the kids want, because now the children are shy and can't say what they want. I stand there like an idiot while everyone has a discussion as what to really get. Several changes occur, the parents order and some more changes are made and now it's done. The children are totally misbehaved and Grandma pretends not to be there and after a major mess on and under the table we are finally done. It's really amazing how some children can't order food when a server is there. It's a $60 check, $10 tip and a huge mess to clean up.

Dealing with kids is fun. Dealing with parents who have no control over their kids, is time consuming and cost the rest of my customers the proper service they deserve. Move on as kids are future customers. I'm sure Grandma was embarrassed, to say the least.

I am a healthy man and have a good appetite, but I cannot eat the way three of my tables did today. At the first table, a slim woman ordered 3 pancakes with walnuts and blueberries and a side of bacon; I can hardly eat two of our pancakes. She also had a soy decaf latté. Her male friend ordered a large fruit bowl to start, large Oatmeal with bananas, raisins, brown sugar and soy milk, followed by an omelet with grits and toast. Oh by the way the man ordered a **pitcher** of water. Ah that's nothing. My very next table was two guys who ordered large oatmeal and a bowl of soup to start, followed by two orders of large berries followed by a Chicken Salad Sandwich with potato chips and six scrambled eggs. The last table was two good looking women in good shape. They both ordered eggs, bacon, home fries and toast and split an order of stuffed pancakes. What good appetites.

I guess as we get older, as I am, we eat less. I can only remember eating like that when I was in high school. I am not and they were not so hats off to large consumption. It created a larger check average than usual. Of course tips are based on check total so I am happy. Happy eating!!

3
Groups

A phone call is made reserving 12 people for 10:00am. This is no problem as I always appreciate the business. This is a chit chat session basically. 9:30am the ladies start to show and order coffee, and hot chocolate, (its 85 degrees down here), but the group spends 50 minutes assembling in my section. As usual I don't have a clue what to expect. Breakfast is ordered and it is pretty simple, served and of course, separate checks. It was a no brainer for the most part, but my question is what the hell they talked about till 1:00pm. Tying up real estate I have talked about in the past, as seats mean money. It's not busy and I really don't care. I worked 13 days in a row and I am really looking forward to having tomorrow off. Tips were awesome and so I have no complaints. However at 11:00am the stations change and the lunch person has no tables as my Church Ladies are still chit chatting, sitting in what was my station and is now hers. The table was bussed to perfection several times as to leave hints to move on, but nothing. I was tempted to mention to them that if they wanted to continue their conversation, maybe they would be more comfortable outside at a patio table, but I didn't. Lunch was slow and I am headed for a day off.

It's hard to ask people to take a hike. My partner had a deuce today and they thought they took up a lot of time at her table and hooked her up with an extra $10. After engaging in a conversation with them after thanking them for the generous tip, they commented that people are not stupid. They do really know they have outstayed their welcome and should accommodate the server for space rental.

It's early Saturday morning and there is not much activity. An elderly lady walks in and tells me there is a party of 8 women that gather monthly and this month they chose us. I'm game and the journey begins. The first two show up for coffee and wait and wait. Two more show and we wait some more. Finally two more show and we order breakfast. Nothing difficult and all goes well. While the chef is doing his thing, two more ladies arrive and I hook them up with breakfast. Now the unexpected 9th person shows and orders a coffee and a muffin. Again it's pretty straightforward.

You guessed it SEPARATE CHECKS!!! Of course I expect this as I always write on my pad in order and seat number or position. After the process is complete I proceed to present the checks and learn that there is more. Number 3, 4, and 5 are on one check. No problem until I dropped the checks and they are wrong. Now I have to figure out what I did wrong and fix it. At this point I'm screwed as the rest of my station is now full and the 10 seats I have on the patio outside are now full. Yearning a cocktail right now I persist. I cruise all my other tables and place orders, refill drinks, etc and return to collect the checks. You guessed it again, lots of credit cards, $20 and $50 bills. Wondering where I left my 9mm handgun, I proceed to be the best, at what I do. Then I finish, bid them farewell, and thank them and wish them back. I am happy now that half of my station is back in service for regular customers after two hours of b#***@!! After posting my tips at the end of the day I see $1.38 $1.50, $1.00, etc, etc. etc. All in all it was about $11.00 for all my frustrations.

I'll shake it off, have a cocktail or 6 and get up tomorrow and do it again. Remember to always use a system for separate checks. I don't care how you do it, circles, arrows, letters or numbers as long as YOU understand it. Doing it all the time makes it easy. Then when you wait on the couple in love for lunch and the request comes for separate checks. You are prepared, because you are the best. If you need help with order taking procedures, let me know and maybe I can help. At least I will try.

You feel like you can do anything after waiting on them, and we usually kick some serious ass on Saturdays.

It's a busy lunch today and a woman calls for a reservation for 8 at noon. I asked what the occasion was it she said it was a birthday. I set the table and the group starts to show up. It consists of 5 Moms, 2 toddlers and three babies. They all arrive at separate times, order at separate times and want separate checks. All these women were beautiful, not only in appearance but in nature. They struggle with highchairs, booster seats, Sippy cups, baby food, DVD movie players and their own special menus and drinks. I give these women credit for going out and struggling with the pleasures of parenting.

Lunch was a success and yes there was a birthday. All goes well and I take my hat off to Moms everywhere who take their little ones out to eat and deal with all the struggles like I remember doing so long ago. Kudos Moms!!

Nine of my new best friends just came in for lunch. It's one o'clock and lunch and my day is about over. I know this is separate checks and I have the only possible spot for a nine top. It's been one hell of a day and I'm ready to go home, but what the hell. I had a little trouble getting to them as I was cleaning up all the details from the noon rush. I approach, greet and apologize for the short wait and told them, they now have my complete attention. I get out my crib sheet and get the order. The boys order out of order, but I am a professional, I know some tricks. I quickly ring in the order as I know the "Day Crew 6am-2pm" will do this one fast as it is probably the last thing they will do before going home. I hustle out the drinks and 12 minutes later, lunch is served. Everything is served in order and after quickly printing the separate checks, I am done. All credit cards, easier than cash as there are no change calculations, receipts are returned for signatures and I am finished. The whole process is less than 45 minutes, start to finish, and the boys were all good to me.

As I said before you can never judge a book by its cover. That's why everyday you start fresh. The guys hooked me up and they were impressed, as one man told the owner, "I'm a keeper". Keep on plugging my friends, some days are just better than others.

There is a ½ marathon in town today and with 3000 participants, you know I'm about to get my ass kicked. Runners have lots of friends so it was a day of large parties (over 10) and a whole lot of separate checks. My first table was 11 people with 7 children all ordering kids pancakes. My second table was thirteen with 9 separate checks. This table was all adults. This is actually pretty simple stuff especially if you have been doing this for a while. Now I am one server out of five. Just try to image, 10 tables consisting of ten people or more, all hitting my little kitchen at the same time. Challenging is not a strong enough word. We succeed. What a day!

Runners are great people. They are very disciplined and their friends have either been there or respect them. They are people of good personal characteristics. They were a pleasure to wait on and good tippers to boot. After all, you couldn't get me to run 13 miles unless I was running to or from something.

Everyone who has been in this business for a while has had the pleasure of waiting on the group from the Tour Bus. It's a package deal including room, tax, transportation, a show and of course dinner. Dinner is a set menu with no exceptions, so let's start. There are 5 vegetarians, two salads no dressing, one salad with dressing on the side, and one meal no sauce. The menu is a mixed grill with tenderloin of beef and sautéed chicken breast, topped with a brown sauce and served with mashed potatoes and asparagus. This meal also includes a mixed green salad, dessert and a choice of soft beverage. Not bad for $14.

Most of these guests are well mannered, well to do and frugal, as beer and wine are extra and only 5 people out of 50 were interested. The meal is served without a hitch and I was only stopped once while clearing plates by an etiquette expert that would not let me take the plates until everyone at the table was done. Let's set the record straight. You are on a schedule, dinner and then a show. You show up a ½ hour late and I don't work at the Waldorf Astoria. Let's hustle people. We move to coffee which can always be a nightmare as no one table wants all regular coffee. We have to split Decafs and regulars only to add a hot tea (decafe of course) to each table. Half and half is not good enough as skim milk and whole milk are required at several tables. This involves many trips to each table. Dessert is next with "I can't eat chocolate", never heard of that as I am a chocolate addict. 9 fresh fruits later and we are done.

It was a lot of work but relatively easy. You do this long enough and shit like this doesn't bother you. You learn to expect the unexpected. Good money for a half day and there will be another tour bus sometime in yours and my future, so suck it up as it's extra money, which in this day and economy is always appreciated.

4

Regulars

It's a Saturday and starting at 8:30 it will start to get busy. We have regular large parties that come in at the same time every week. We start with the Bridge Runners at 8:30, 6-9 people, AKA the oatmeal kids as 75% of them order oatmeal. They are easy as they all drink coffee, no need to even ask. They are followed by the Decafe Kids. Usually 6-8 people and all but one drinks Decafe. They are followed by the YMCA boys. There is 8-12, every week after their work-out at the gym. These guys come in all the time and are a piece of cake. Half order Granola and the rest order straight off the menu. They all have separate checks, we know all their names and usually what they order. We make them feel like part of our family and they make us feel like part of theirs. It's a good feeling.

It really is a good feeling when a large group walks in and everybody knows **_your_** name. That's what called "Doing it Right". I love working Saturdays as these customers get us going and set the tone for the day.

Everyone loves a good massage. That's how Licensed Massage Therapists make a living, making us feel great. I have met many, at my restaurant and they all have a common dominator. They are all super nice people. How can that be? Is there a "Nice Person 101 Class" that they are required to take before they get their license or is it some trait in people who want to become LMTs? There is something special about LMTs as they are always a pleasure to wait on, very polite and good tippers.

I met an entertainer a few weeks ago. She was the nicest person. We had a good intelligent conversation for about an hour after her performance and when I asked what her day job was she said, LMT. Hmmm! My massages in the past were always a positive experience and my 2nd ex-wife was a massage therapist. I work with someone who used to be LMTs. Oh My God they are everywhere! Something about people wanting to make other people feel better shows how big their hearts are.

Remember to love your massage therapist as they have the biggest hearts of all. I met a LMT in training today and she is looking for a practice subject. I am there and it's free to boot. Hey a practice massage is better than no massage at all. Feel better my friends. Relax and enjoy!

Tennis is a very popular sport for all ages in Florida, so I see a lot of players. It's a sport you can play till you die, because after you pass middle age, you switch from playing single matches to playing double matches. In the middle the week, in the middle of the morning and sitting in the middle of my patio, sit the nicest group of tennis girls I have ever encountered. They are all smartly dressed in tennis attire and they are older, (have been collecting Social Security for a while). It's a bunch of work as they have Skinny Lattes, Skinny Cappuccinos, Skinny Decaf Lattes and Cappuccinos and I have to write this beverage order down to get it right. Most of them eat light, muffins, bagels, oatmeal and only one of the 12, orders a meal. We take good care of them and it's a positive event for everyone. They tip well, pay with credit cards (easier than cash), and a pleasure to wait on.

Take care of regulars like these girls and other I have talked about. As you can tell, all these regulars (large parties) build your customer base which makes you money all year and during the off season.

Two Gents show up on a slow Saturday and say there might be nine. Inside or out I ask, and they reply I don't know. They park in my section while they wait outside and I am thrilled that they are mine as it has been Dead Slow thus far. After all, how hard can this be? The others show up and now it's is eleven and they take two tables, one of five and one of six. I inquire about the nature of their visit and they respond that they have nothing better to do. Obviously this is a group of senior men that go around town and terrorize restaurants and see who will invite them back. First question, separate checks and the answer is yes. It seems pretty simple as all except but one is drinking coffee, one person is always drinking Hot Tea, you know , an underliner, pot of water, lemon wedge and a separate cup and of course one of the 20 flavors of tea bags. There is always one.

I am a genius as I decide to ring the two tables separately as it's easier for me and the kitchen won't get a mile long ticket. This is great. The orders are straight forward and it's done. Food is out, checks are separated and on the table. Here comes the nightmare, wait for it, wait for it, and wait for it. I start processing checks and some of the gentlemen are buying for others. Not too bad except I cannot find the other orders on the table. Three gents are buying breakfast for gents at the other table. My POS system doesn't like this. This requires lots of voiding, re-ringing and don't making for the kitchen. Of course now I am busy as the entire restaurant is full. Now I am not giving the kind of service everyone deserves because I am dealing with this nonsense. It was a very intense 18 minutes.

We are never too old to learn. One check next time, not two, is better. You never know when this will happen again. I enjoy waiting on all kinds of people in all kinds of situations. I do not enjoy taking my valuable time performing accounting functions because it was not separate checks, it was cluster checks. Learn and move on. They come back on a regular basis now and we don't display attitudes or frustration toward them, regardless how much paperwork is involved, we are happy to have them.

5

Favorite Guests

My favorite part about this job is the regular guests that come in so frequently I consider them my friends. We say hello, call each other my name and shake hands on the way in and on the way out. It's a good feeling. This place has a "Cheers" affect, where everyone likes to go where everybody knows you name.

First is Lee who never misses a day unless he is out of town. In his seventies and retired, he comes in to interact with the crew. We talk politics when he is there as we follow some of the same TV shows mostly on Fox News. He is a big Bill O'Reilly fan as am I. Next would be Max. He is a retired Pharmacist who has stopped looking for work and is on a limited income. He is the nicest guy in the world. He listens to all the conversations that the staff has behind the bar and understands what's going on in the restaurant more than some employees do. Then there is Tim. He is not only a regular nighttime patron and Sunday morning, but he is also my neighbor. He builds fountains and pools for the rich and famous, has to have his half and half out of the jug and is a super tipper. Let's talk about

Keith. He owns the Gym in the next building and works in a similar line of work as Tim. He is a great guy, as we go out with him and his wife from time to time as we have become friends. There is Ronnie, Antonio, Marty, Harold and the rest of the finance boys. They come in and have meetings some days at separate tables with a mix and match lineup of attendees. I 'm not sure exactly what they do but it always sounds important.

What all these regulars have in common is intelligence and respect. Maybe it's the intelligence part that allows them to show us tremendous respect. We are servers but we are the best around and they recognize us for that. They don't treat us like second class citizens like a lot of our customers do. We return the respect with warm greeting, prompt service and use their names usually in a pretty loud voice as they love hearing the sound of their names and it makes them feel important. They enjoy that. It's a mutual respect.

A gorgeous red-head (everyone knows I love red-heads) and another older, attractive woman are doing lunch today. They are probably 50 and 60 years old respectfully. They both have great personalities and are very friendly. The red-head is waiting for her friend and we chit chat for a while as it is not very busy today. Her friend arrives and when I approach to take the order I overhear part of the ordering decision. The older woman said the last time she had Eggs Benedict it was three in the morning. She busted me listening and I just raised my eyebrows. She offered to tell me it was after dancing all night. She then asked me if I liked to dance. I explained that my parents taught all of us kids to dance every Sunday after church. It always came in handy at weddings and always helped out while dating. Women love men who know how to move. This innocent flirting goes on throughout lunch and some unspoken thoughts are transmitted non-verbally and the whole lunch was a good time for all of us.

I don't know if either one of us could cut a rug like we used to. I can't help thinking that 30 years ago; it would have been one hell of a night. I love my job!

A whole bunch of really cool customers dined with me today. They were very understanding, pleasant, impressed and decent tippers. I had a lot of brand new people in today who were very impressed as how good their first visit was. A lot were surprised that we could fulfill their special orders and were impressed by food service times today. The kitchen was on fire today, not literally. I had people ask for exceptions and actually told me "you can charge me extra". One man suggested to his wife to upgrade to fruit instead of home fries. He said, it says here in the menu it's only $1.49. Wow, someone actually read that. I know it's in the middle of the menu, but no one remembers seeing it when they get the bill. Everyone was happy today and not one complaint. What a great day! The "Man on Fire" was turning tables, "Turn & Burn", and just cruising to the finish line.

These days are uplifting and it is also nice to tell you about the good days as opposed to the many challenging days. As I am just back from my road trip, it was nice to get back in the saddle.

I have learned over the years that Mimosa people are cool and great tippers. Three younger people enter the restaurant and sit at the bar (counter). They order three Mimosas. I say younger as 40 is probably the average age of most of our patrons and I am guessing these guests are in their mid-twenties. I didn't wait on them but I love the freestyle life of having mimosas before noon and not having anything important to do for the rest of the day. The next thing I noticed was they parked themselves outside in my patio section and I think it was just to smoke some cigarettes. It's not busy and I am not concerned. I approach and inquire if I can help and they state they are waiting for others to have lunch. They order 2 more mimosas and a coffee and water. They are very friendly and we connect right away with some bad jokes and some light humorous bantering. The group continues to grow, ordering more mimosas and now the party peaks at the number 7.

Now it is time to take the order and I have to ask the all important question, Separate Checks? But of course. They inform me they are all separate but guest 1 is buying a mimosa for number 5 and for number 7 and he would like one more. They continue to order, one by one, special requests, 3 extra sides of bacon in addition to the bacon that comes with, add a coffee, and add a large OJ and two more mimosas. It took 2 pages on the little order pad to get the order and sort out the drinks but, I got it! Oh and can #4 get a cup of coffee? Order placed and food served with PERFECTION.

Now splitting the check is easy if you do it my way. I ring the drinks with the food instead of separately. Then when I split the check, I just go down the line, touch drinks and food and done. Print, 7 checks and present. I thought I had it but I got one cup of coffee wrong. I guess there is nothing wrong with 99%. Got the mimosas right, which was the most confusing part. I told them I would write about them in this Blog as they really were a fun group. I receive 6 credit cards and one cash payment and the girls tells me to keep the change.

It's toward the end of my shift, it's been nuts all day, one server short and this is how my day will end, so I have to use the cash tip as an indicator. 50% tip. Yeah! I process the six credit cards and return them for signatures and tips. I am pleasantly surprised. 2 more 50%, 2- 30% tips and one guy who didn't get it, at 20%. Hey $50 on $130 check. This is a great way to end a shift.

Look at mimosa people with great respect. They order cocktails at breakfast time. They are fun to wait on and oh, GREAT TIPPERS. I almost forgot about the separate checks. Of course we servers all know that the worst day at work can always replaced by a big pile of cash.

A young couple sits on the patio for breakfast. The woman is young, attractive and has hair the color of Paprika. They look like a nice couple and they order breakfast. He has water and she orders a Cappuccino. It's a fairly standard deal and some extra work is required for a second cappuccino, a to-go box, a pastry bag, and a to-go cup, all separate requests and separate trips. I love redheads and the fair skin look of these women, even though I have never married one. Some say redheads have a unique personality and I would agree, but I love them just the same. Maybe I pay a little extra attention to them and that may be to their advantage, service wise. I enjoyed our time together, only to be disappointed by the 10% tip.

I will still pay more attention to redheads as it is my right to dream a little. I am certain the boyfriend paid the tip. The redhead is off the hook for being a cheapskate.

6

Difficult Guests

It was a steady lunch today after a "Crushing" Sunday. I'm a little tired after celebrating my birthday yesterday but I'm okay. A couple comes in today at 12:30 and they are in a hurry. They ask if it's possible to get in and out in 30 minutes. We are a full service restaurant but I have been working here what seems like forever and I figure this is very possible. I assure them it's no problem. I do my magic and lunch is on the table in 8 minutes. Now all they have to do is eat it. The check is already on the table. They are very impressed that I kept my promise and expressed their appreciation for helping them achieve their goal. They leave the money on the table, thank me again and say "great job" and depart for their appointment.

It's what we do. I know our capabilities and what we can and cannot do. I run over to bus the table and open the check presenter and find a $20 bill to cover an $18.16 check. A disappointing $1.84 tip is left to cover a special need. I tell myself I've stopped worrying about the little things as all the stains usually come out in the wash. It was still a great weekend and a great birthday.

A young couple comes in today and the female decides she wants a Greek Wrap for breakfast. The Greek Wrap includes black olives, spinach, tomatoes and Feta Cheese in a tortilla wrap. She however wants to change the wrap into a breakfast sandwich. I agree and we continue with what she wants. She doesn't want the wrap obviously but wants it on an English muffin. She doesn't want the Feta cheese. I ask her to stop and tell her to tell me what she DOES want and I can make it happen for her (very accommodating).

She explains she doesn't want any cheese and instead of tomatoes she wants mushrooms. I reiterate. I have connected with this couple now as I look at the male and ask him "how he does it?" They both laugh and we start over. We end up with a breakfast sandwich with scrambled eggs with spinach, black olives and mushrooms on an English muffin. The male orders something straight off the menu and off I go. I order the food and chat with the chef to make sure we are on the same page. The food comes out and everything is perfect and the female is ecstatic. Good job!

I am certain you cannot get this Egg McMuffin extraordinaire at MacDonald's. I don't know but sometimes I wonder if people think we used pre-packaged food. We make everything from scratch, everytime. It's no big deal if you just tell me WHAT you want.

My regular Bridge Runners come in and the old challenge of separate checks is back in play. 14 today is the lucky number with only three couples. So it is 9 separate checks. Here is the twist. They all arrive and eat at separate times. So it is also true they will pay and depart at separate times. The task is to split off separate people, issue their checks, cash them out and then add more food, resplit the remaining checks, etc, etc, etc.. The cycle just keeps repeating itself. I used the same check nine different times. All goes well as there isn't much else going on at this time, yet!

I love a good challenge and achieving perfection should be everyone's goal. I just can't imagine what else they can throw at me. I love this guys and I certainly hope they love me. See you guys next week!

I really hate working weekends. All the amateur tippers come in and make demands before they screw you. A couple arrives wearing, probably $300 worth of biking gear and grab a table outside, which is cool because they most likely have been sweating because they rode 10 miles to get here. They order things like HOT Lattes, DRY toast, Egg Whites, FRESH SQUEEZED orange juice and anything else they can do, to try to trip you up and try to complain. They order like that because somewhere 20 years ago someone told them eggs, butter, concentrated orange juice and tepid Lattes are bad for you. They probably are sporting a 10% body fat and have a heart stronger than an ox. They treat you like you are there to serve them and I am, it's just their tone in their voices I don't care for. So every effort is made to make it perfect, so they have nothing to complain about. I succeed. They're disappointed as they cannot find anything to complain about, which is some people's goal in life. The check is presented and is carefully reviewed for mistakes and wondering what all the upcharges are for.

Lattes are more expensive than coffee and egg whites are extra. They finally figure out how to meet their budget for breakfast. Their $15 breakfast is now $20. They leave $22 and head for the bikes. They required no change and pay in cash and make sure I don't get a chance to count the cash to see how they screwed me. They say thank you, not meaning it, as they climb on their $800 bikes and depart the premises.

Just realize that some people have their financial priorities messed up. They will spend thousands of dollars on their biking equipment, their dogs, clothes, jewelry and other things and yet have no regard for the hard working server, with a kid in college, who just jumped through hoops to get them the meal exactly the way they wanted it. Learn to live with it as the difference is made up by the Mimosa people and your regulars who hook you up on a daily basis.

Some people just shouldn't leave the house. If I am ever in a bad mood, I try to stay home. If I must go out, I try to be as reserved as possible around people so I don't project my foulness. However, some folks either don't have enough sense to stay home or have no clue how bitchy they come off. I hear staff all day refer to these guests, in a complaining fashion, in their native language and some foreign languages. For example; they will ask for coffee, when you return with it, they ask for skim milk on the side, and then ask for iced water when you return with the skim milk. The whole meal is like this. Their attitude and there tone is negative and something we don't need to hear or put up with. After all, whatever your problem is, I can assure you we probably had nothing to do with it. They are also, in most cases the worst tippers, thinking 10% is ok. We have some finicky regulars and I don't mind a little running and ass kissing, because I know they are decent tippers.

As it said in one of our on-line reviews said "Loose the Tude". If you are going to come in and give us attitude, then stay at home. If you do go out and come to visit me, then please be polite and be on your best behavior. We would all appreciate it. Thank you.

Is the use of your cell phone in a restaurant just rude or just stupid? Correct me if I'm wrong. You wouldn't have a conversation on your cell phone if you were talking to your spouse, your boss or your kids. So why would you talk on your cell phone when you go to a restaurant to eat? If you are talking on your cell phone in my section, I will not recognize that you are there, until you get off the phone. Don't try to squeeze me in for the drink order or wait until the other party is talking so you can order your food. I am on a schedule and am not going to wait for an opportunity to wait on you.

You need my services if you are hungry and I have plenty of other stuff to do while you are being rude. Do not look at me when you do get off the phone, like you've have been here forever either. Another question I have is, "Why do we all have to listen to your end of the conversation and why are you talking so loud?" Is your cell service that bad that you need to talk that loud?

I know a convenience store that has a sign that says they will not wait on you if you are on your phone, please step out of line. Telling people to hold on, is a good option. I had a woman experience her entire meal from start to finish while on her phone. If you want to talk, stay outside and talk. If you want to eat, come on in, you're welcome, just stay off your phone.

Everyday people come in and ask us for things we do not have, or expect we would carry. If you want waffles, go to The Waffle House, French fries; go to McDonalds, Ice cream; Big Olaf's, Almond milk; go to a health food store. If you would not expect to have it in your house, don't expect me to have it here. If you want an Iced Caramel Macchiato, go to Starbucks. Someone once asked me if we serve eggs, (strange question for a breakfast restaurant). We do listen to customer requests and try to accommodate whenever we can. We have brought in products after several requests, which unfortunately are followed by complaints for charging extra. We need to charge extra for special items, as they cost more than the normal items designed in the menu. Ounce for ounce Gluten Free Bread, for example, is $11.00 compared to $1.50 for a regular loaf of bread.

We could give you a choice of all these special items as part of our menu, but every entree would be priced upward and that would scare our non-special guests away. Please try to find something comparable on our menu and please don't take your disappointment out on the server's tip. They have nothing to do with it.

Two women in for the lunch rush needed a minute to look at the menu. This is never a problem as I always have other stuff to do. I return and they claim they are ready. They inquire about items that are not on the menu as one is a vegetarian. I make some suggestions but they still are unsure. They ask some questions and I suggest they should tell me what they really want and I can make it happen. We begin to create a Veggie Sandwich and then change it to a half sandwich with a cup of soup, then to a half sandwich and a salad. Not liking the salad choices more changes come. Her guest, now realizing you can get a salad and half sandwich changes her order. While these women are changing their mind several times I can feel the rest of the people in my station needing me, (the other stuff I need to do). I scrap the current page on my note book and start over as it is now illegible with changes. The vegetarian changes her order completely now to a regular menu item, Hmm? The order is done and 6 minutes has past. Six more minutes has past and they have food and are happy. It's interesting that it takes as much time to make your food as it did for you to decide what you wanted.

Six minutes is a huge amount of time to spend at one table (of two) during the lunch hour. It takes away from the service I can give the rest of my customers. I wait on an average of 45-60 people during the lunch rush. If you are still not ready to order then tell me, and I will come back. Remember I always have other stuff to do!

It's been raining for days and our Doggie Dining feature is used by canine lovers frequently. We get them water, feed them biscuits and show a lot of attention to man's best friend. Could you possibly be so inconsiderate of your server, who will have to dodge rain drops while you sit under your umbrella, while your dog is getting wet, who really doesn't care? I guess you were made for each other. So while I am running in and out of a hot kitchen to get your food, an air-conditioned dining room, and out to you so you can be with your friend, you still leave me 15% for my service. The least you could do is think about leaving me another $5 so I can get some Nyquil to treat the cold I going to get for the next two days.

I'll give you some advice, which I don't normally do. The next time you are hungry and it is raining, LEAVE THE DOG HOME!!

Like most days, some couple will come in with no personal skills whatsoever. It always starts out with my upbeat friendly greeting. "Good Morning, how are you today". There is no response. This is pretty much like ignoring someone when they say "Hello". Now that the tone is set, I know what to expect. Conversation will be minimal and they most likely are looking for something to be wrong (an excuse not to tip well). Now that we know that, "Let's Smoke em"! Let's do everything extra perfect so there is no reason to complain. Be attentive, accurate and basically kiss some ass. I don't know what made these people this way, but they are usually non-responsive to all questions, more coffee, a signal, not words. How is everything? They pretend to be eating and you get a nod, again no words. Good tips are not expected in these situations, but you have to give it your best. It could be a relationship thing or just the way they are. It's sad that people can't be polite and at least cordial. Just short of being rude, they and you make it through. Who cares what the tip was as long as they leave.

Maybe they don't realize how they are acting or they think you are only a server and find no need to communicate with you due to your profession. I move on because I am always cordial and polite wherever I go and I live with the philosophy, no one should be treated like shit.

Today lunch was slow but it was a day of exceptions (make your own menu). There is a rule of thumb to follow while dining out. If you order something that deviates from the menu and the chef has never made this before, the odds are he might not get it right. As opposed to ordering something on the menu the way it was intended, the odds are that after making it 5000 times, it will be perfect. I had two women today who were amazing. The first lady, no not Michelle Obama, ordered a Spinach Salad, and then removed everything that came with it, except the spinach, then added Feta cheese and grilled fish. The second lady ordered a Mediterranean Salad, and then took off 60% of what came on it, i.e. No Onions, No Olives, and No Peperoncini and then added blackened chicken. Guess what, the kitchen got it wrong. Both ladies wanted dressing on the side with no toast, gluten free folks. What a day!

I love to make people happy and exceptions never bother me, but let's look at this. There were12 exceptions on two salads, REALLY. I only had nine tables for lunch and each one was close to the same with the exception thing. The chef spent more time reading exceptions than he did cooking. Oh well, tomorrow is another day.

It's not worth what is used to be but that's a different story. Paying a $20 breakfast check with a hundred dollar bill at 8:30am on a weekend is a pain in the ass. If you needed to break it, you should have thought about that on Friday before the bank closed. Servers carry about $20 cash for change on a daily basis. Breaking a hundred is difficult. Maybe you are trying to impress someone (a date) or impress me. I scurry and make the change and the couple says everything was great. The restaurant was full and they were impressed as to how fast they were in and out. Paying an $80 dinner bill with a hundred and telling the server to keep the change is impressive. Leaving me $2 on a $20 breakfast bill is not. Was your date impressed because I sure was not?

Life will go on and $50 and $100's fly all the time. We do our best to accommodate. People who are not in this business do not think of things like, maybe they won't have change this early in the morning. This guy obviously didn't know how to tip either. Next time, go to the supermarket and buy a dozen eggs with your hundred dollar bill and stay home and make breakfast. You also won't have to part with that $2 tip.

People in this world and I'm not sure what percentage it is, are out to beat the system. I knew a waiter who once who bought a stack of newspapers everyday to use the $10.00 off coupons in the restaurant during a summer promotion. When anyone paid cash he would pull out a coupon and present it to the cashier, a recently lost occupation, but the story, not the concept is old. We had to make it policy for a manager to visit every table with a coupon.

Living Social is a great product for businesses to promote themselves. At a one day sale we sold over 1000 coupons for a cost of $15.00, good for a value of $30.00. Great deal Huh? Present the coupon and get thirty dollars credit, gratuity not included. Good promotion for our summer slump. One customer bought ten. Then Mr. Beat the System shows up. Young man, beautiful wife and 2 lovely children, eats, uses the coupon and pays the difference and departs. Three days later he brings a photocopy of the same coupon to use it again. This man bought two coupons. Using a photocopy, and realizing how busy the lunch rush is, he pulls it off. At the end of the day, while posting the coupons to the master list we discover the coupon has been used before. I applied his photocopy to his other coupon, as they are numbered. My guess is he will try to use his other coupon as well as a copy of the second one.

I have alerted the staff, as I know in the middle of lunch it is difficult to go to the master list, but if you get a photocopy, stop what you are doing and look it up. You can get me because I am waiting for this guy.

7

Tipping

I will review the five types of tippers;

1. The Moron; this individual has no clue what tipping is about. They look at it as an unnecessary expense. They dine out frequently but should stay at home more often. 10% or less is this tipper, and they don't feel bad, they don't know how to tip the pizza delivery people or cab drivers either.
2. The Conservative; this individual has no idea how hard servers and bartenders work. They think it's easy, although they have never done or could never do it. 10-15% if you're lucky. They usually look for a reason not to leave a decent tip. Things like buffet service, bad food, (but don't complain), or slow timing because they didn't allow themselves enough time for the meal. These are the things that go through their heads when calculating the tip.
3. Average Joe; this individual is everywhere and that's we why we make a good living. They know what

we do, how hard we work and tip accordingly, and 15-20%. This is most likely 80% of people.
4. The Flasher; this individual wants to be noticed and catered to. They have aggressive personalities, have bucks, and are generally on the ball in every social category. Recognize the Flasher, kiss some butt and make some money, Yeah! 20%+
5. Hospitality People; these individuals are **US!** These individuals are in the business or have been. They compliment you when you are busy and they are sympathetic when you are slammed. They know the crap you put up with everyday and they tip very generously. I got a Christmas tip once from a server, $20 tip, on a $20 check. I have also left 30%, 50%, and 100% as tips before. It makes a servers day and it's only money.

Realize that you are not going to change the way people tip. All you can ever do is your best. At the end of each day it all works out well. Some days are just better than others.

If the establishment would pick up the 5% difference between the "used to be" and the "supposed to be" tip, a servers' job would be more sought after, respected, and higher paying. That would attract better employees and create longevity in each restaurant. Let me talk about the differences between the time when 15%, was the "suppose to be" tip and now. During 15% I paid $1.70 for a gallon of gasoline, I now pay $4.00. I used to pay $3.00 for a pound of coffee, now I pay $6.50. My co-pay at my Primary care Physicians' office used to be $10, I now pay $35. When I used to smoke, cigarettes were $3.00, now in Florida they are $7.00 a pack. So while I pay $50 to fill up my car, $9.00 for a can of coffee and have a $35.00 co-pay at the doctors' office, most customers are still leaving 15%.

So to adjust for the problem, tomorrow I am going to drive less, drink less coffee at home, see the doctor less times per year and I already quit smoking. So while you drive your gas guzzling SUV, pay $80.00 per gallon for Starbucks, and send your kids to private schools. I WILL still be here.

In these times of economic hardship, one should never assume anything when it comes to money. In my job, I never assume I am getting a huge tip or I am getting screwed. With two credit cards in one checkbook, can one assume they want the bill split in half or do they want it split in detail as not previously requested? A cash payment of $22.00 on a $21.09 check, I will assume they are not leaving me a 91¢ tip, so I give them change. This is just a reminder that you are NOT leaving me 91¢. I assumed once on a $22.00 check with

$25.00 in the book that I was to keep the change. Wrong. The customer then asked where his change was and left me a $2.00 tip. Boo Hoo! The term when someone says "All Set" in my book means keep the change. This is not always true. A fellow server picked up a checkbook last week with cash and a credit card in it. She did not look or inquire and just gave me the book. I assumed, like in most cases, a lot of people don't like charging tips, so they leave cash and put the meal on the card. That's what I did; I did not count the money and made an incorrect assumption. A $25.00 check with $12.00 cash in it did not mean I was getting a 50% tip, it meant $12.00 cash and the rest on the card. My bad! I got called on it by the guest, who should have instructed the server as what to do. No harm done, but the ladies were overheard saying they didn't believe me when I told her I didn't count the cash. Hey, it was lunch hour and I was busy.

When picking up a checkbook, always look inside and ask for directions. I picked up a book once and looked inside and there wasn't enough money to cover the bill. It's best to find out before you leave the table.

I have noticed a pattern in tipping percentages since we have gone to off season hours. This means less server coverage as sometimes there is only one server. This particular morning I got slammed 2 minutes before opening. I ran like a mad man for an hour taking care of everyone's needs. Due to the off season there is NO support before 9:00am. So, like Tom Hanks, in "Castaway", there is no help in sight, for the first ninety minutes. After two weeks into the summer program now, I have found that my tip percentage is so much higher during that time frame, than the rest of the week. Do people tip you more because they see you are slammed as opposed to a regular day where you have time to chit-chat with people and it appears you are not working as hard? It seems so.

The service is the same less the chit-chat. You can't help but looked swamped. It worked for me today again.

All this time I have been getting it wrong. The standard for tipping is really 15%. I thought it was 20% but that is a mistake. Twenty percent is the average that I make almost every day. Therefore, the average person is actually very appreciative when they tip 15% because they feel they have received great service. I discovered this in the past few weeks when the new edition of Living Social vouchers hit the street. The value is $30 and they paid $15. Most people leave $5. That is actually 16.7%. So I will remove the disappointment from my life and learn to expect less. I will still average over 20% and just be more appreciative of the exceptional people who leave 20% or more.

I will lower my expectations for all people now which will enable me to have a more positive feeling about tipping in general and suffer less disappointment. Let's just say, I will look at my glass as being half full as opposed as being half empty.

It is 9:00am and a reservation of 12 is scheduled to arrive and the necessary arrangements have been made. Its summer and it's always nice to have extra business as in Florida, September is the slowest time of the year. The first guest arrives and inquires as to how many high chairs we have. Oh No!! I reply" three" and over the next half hour the rest of the group shows up. I take the drink orders, one at a time, as that's how they arrived, consisting of lots of iced water, skinny lattes, decafs with soy milk and a soy milk Cappuccino. So far, a lot of work has been done just to get through the beverage portion of this order. Then the food, a kid's pancake and three plates then stop, we'll wait.

Keeping my smile and composure, I continue to wait on the rest of my customers and return to get the breakfast order. All the time, I remind you I'm thinking $100 check and a $20 tip. I take the food order which consist of 2 egg orders, 2 bagels, one side of fruit, one pancake, Buckwheat of course, and an order of oatmeal. Dollarwise it was a little disappointing. I relentlessly cater to their needs with refills, to-go cups and to-go containers. Good news one check. It was a lot of work for a $44.00 check.

Lesson for today is never show your game face. Positive attitude is what we do. A poor attitude would send this group of 12 elsewhere next time they got together. Always keep your head up and remember "never judge a book by its cover". By the way, they left a $20.00 tip. You never know.

I realized how leaving your servers bigger tips, can help turn the economy around. I will explain. If your server makes more money every day, then they traditionally will stop for more cocktails on the way home, more nights per week. We all know that servers are the best tippers so now the bartenders are making more money. Let's just say most of the bartenders can now afford a bigger and better TV. They go out and buy an "American made" product like Vizio, Westinghouse or Element.

Well here is the effect. The bars all across America will have to hire more bartenders to handle more business. The retail stores will have to increase their sales staff for all the additional TV sales. The manufacturers will have to hire more workers to assemble the TVs' and maybe even build new plants to handle the huge increase in sales (hopefully stealing sales from TVs made in other countries). Now we have to hire more construction workers to build these new facilities. Works for me!

So the next time you go out for a meal and you get your check, you have to decide how much tip to leave. Think about how you can help get this country's economy back on track again.

It's a Saturday afternoon and 6 people walk in and asked to have the one TV we have to be tuned to a college game of their choice. Owners orders, its news and weather only. We are not a sports bar with 20 TV's and every time we put a game on, as soon as we change it, there is a major problem. My partner, after I explain the policy, changes the channel anyway. I explain that I am not taking the heat on this one if the owner walks in. A young lady from this group comes to me and hands me a credit card to insure there in no scuffle over who is paying the bill. The meal is served with perfection and on a timely basis and one older woman orders Blintzes to-go. This is an item not normally available. I comply and give her a great price. Added to the check and jumping through hoops, i.e. game and blintzes, the young lady hands the credit card slip to an older gentleman. He adds 15%, you are kidding. It's an $86.00 check and a $12.00. Come again real soon. It makes me not want to do shit for people. Learn how to show appreciation.

It is my conclusion that older people still think a good tip is 15%. 10 to 15 years ago yeah! Younger people always seem to tip better and they realize that we only make $4.00 per hour. Keep your head up as it all seems to average out over time.

An Eighteen top scheduled to arrive at 9:00am and no idea what to expect. Two show up and wait 20 minutes, then two more and 10 minutes later 2 more. My entire section now reconstructed into this eighteen top and the six decide to order. The order consists of one Bagel with no cream cheese, one small oatmeal and a small granola. Everyone else is drinking coffee or iced tea. Wow. While I place the order two more ladies arrive only to add a large oatmeal and a decaf. I fetch the oatmeal and number nine shows up for a muffin and coffee and that is it. It's a $44.00 check and there are nine no shows and one more hour for a meeting.

The good news is one check with a $20 tip. Never judge a book by its cover. I'll move on.

School is out for spring break and maybe this is a week where people who don't normally eat out, do. Mom, who appears to be in her mid to late thirties, and two teenage boys, say 12 and 15, come in for breakfast. They appear to be in a huge hurry. This is no problem as it is dead slow at this hour. They order drinks and food all at the same time. I place the order and bring the drinks. Food comes out fast and I place the check on the table, making the local drive-thru look slow. I'm thinking job well done and so does Mom. She left a $2 tip on a $20 check. Like I said, probably don't go out much.

Later the same morning, three eastern Europeans come in. It's still quiet. They are well mannered, well dressed and very polite. They order breakfast and everything is perfect as usual. The check is $20.50 and there is $22.00 in the check presenter. I figure they need change because I am sure they are not going to leave me $1.50. By returning the change, it reminds them exactly how much they are leaving me, in case they have miscalculated. It works! However not to my satisfaction, they threw in an extra buck.

Let's see now. $2.50 on $20.50, that's a 12.2% tip, coupled with the 10% with the mom and two boys, made for a discouraging morning. Luckily the rest of the day kicked ass and the total day was not a loss. Poor tippers are not your fault. There is a lot of ignorance in the world. Tomorrow is another and better day.

Someone decided a long time ago to change the average expected tip for _good service_ from 15% to 20%. Private Clubs started this because they want to be able to attract and maintain a higher quality wait staff for longer periods of time. By taking the service charge up, it puts more responsibility on the guests (members) and less financial responsibility on the employer. The restaurant industry followed suit soon thereafter. Some private clubs are up to 24% gratuity. Now that the standard for the expected tip for _good service_ is 20% and not 15%, I ask the question, how come so many people didn't get the memo? I watch people calculate tips every day. They carry the 1 and round off to the nearest dollar. I see people use their IPods', cell phones and their noggins to calculate the tip. It's simple, multiply the total X 2 and drop a zero. I can do that in my head. It's much harder to figure 15%. I looked up some cell phone apps for figuring the tip and all the default setting are set to 15%. The IT people are not helping me out here. Remember you still have the right to lower the tip for inadequate service and you can always over tip for service like mine, great or perfect.

I am now going to send an email to everyone in the world and let them know the new standard is and has been 20%. Maybe some people will catch up on bad tipping (doubt it). Next I am going to hack every app for smart phones and change the default setting to 20% and you will have to be an IT genius to go into setting, tools, configuration, etc, etc to change it to anything else but 20%. Hang in there my friends. We will get there.

Four people dressed in scrubs are in for lunch today and decided to sit outside. After doing this for a while you can easily figure out who goes out to eat frequently and who doesn't. These folks must have been brown baggers forever. I don't like people who go out to eat and try to save money at the same time as you and I both know where the savings are coming from, my tip. There are three women and one man. The man orders a bottle of water and a muffin at the take-out counter because he figures he won't have to leave a tip. The three women go outside and proceed to order three iced waters and look at menus. Iced water is my first clue as to the fact they don't want to pay $2.00 for a beverage. It takes three more trips outside in the Florida sun for them to decide what to order.

Each time I go out to get the order I overhear them discussing the prices. I am destined for doom. They finally order and prompt and efficient service follows as everything is perfect. Separate checks are issued and debit cards are presented for payment. All the checks are about the same amount $9.00. As I look at the tips I ask myself this question, "Don't most people confer with each other when deciding how much of a tip to leave?" I do all the time. It's a simple question, "what are you leaving him?" One leaves me $3.00, one leaves $1.25 and the other leaves $0. We already know the guy who ordered at the take-out counter has left zero.

Ignorance is bliss. Ignorance is no excuse. Ignorance is costing me money. If you don't know how to do something well, then you should refrain from doing it. Obviously these people should stick to brown-bagging it.

8

Complaints

It was a busy Sunday after church today and things turned out well. My five table station filled up all at once and it was no problem as during the week I have twice as many tables. I retrieve drinks, place food orders and everything is great. Separate checks are issued to a four top and single checks are issued to the rest of my station. Everyone leaves and life is good. Four of my five tables are impressed with the speed of service as no one has been there 40 minutes. That's not bad on a Sunday with a ten minute wait for a table. However, perception is what appears to be, not what actually is. It's what you make your mind believe. The four top made a written comment on the guest check that the service was slow. I guess it was their perception, that with the wait for the table, the loud volume in the restaurant and witnessing everyone running around, you thought service was bad. Look at the clock!

So 16 people were pleased and you were not. I am not supposed to say that the four individual checks slowed me down because it didn't. So why the comment? Was it ignorance or just an excuse to beat up an old man? These are the types of people who will go online and lodge a complaint, list my name and hopefully get me canned. And I say "Sweetheart, come and do my job on a Sunday and then we'll talk!"

Two women claimed to experience a 90 minute lunch, never has happened and never will happen. People who write reviews and post them online have a tendency to exaggerate. Two women come in for lunch and wrote a review stating that it took 30 minutes to get their order taken and another 30 minutes to get their food. I have been their over three years and trust me, there is no way possible that this would happen. First of all, we have the fastest kitchen I have ever worked in. Second, if I had to wait 30 minutes to have my order taken, I would walk out. They also stated that it appeared that I was not too keen about waiting on two women. Anyone who knows me knows I love waiting on women as I would prefer to only wait on women.

Before you write a review for the entire world to see on the internet, get your facts straight. You obviously did not try to get anyone's attention and did not complain while you were there. Therefore I feel you have no right to bash the establishment and me. The restaurant could suffer a loss of customers based on your "review" and you certainly put my job in jeopardy as my boss reads all the reviews and I am the only male server in the house. I suggest you find something better to do with your free time.

Let's talk about complaints, service complaints. Have you ever gone in a bar for the first time and everyone there, except you, was a regular. Not a great feeling unless you are a genuine hermit. This is about me and my complaints and yes I get my share. Lately though, the last complaint was I didn't treat people in my station like regulars. You know them, what they drink, what they eat and know their names. This translated to me being rude to those who felt left out, like the bar. I actually had customers the other day, who after my pleasant professional greeting responded, "They haven't fired you yet?" Of course my response was, "Not yet but any day now, keep sending those emails", and continued to take the order. I am confused by this comment as to his level of seriousness. Was he joking or was he actually serious and the same person who wrote an email about me being "rude?

It puzzles me and I thought about it two nights, didn't lose any sleep, but I wondered. Let's remember that in life, it is not what is, but it is what is perceived. If I am perceived as being Rude, and guest continues to write emails, I could get fired, weather I am rude or not. What a quandary. In recent days a few comments were made and I wondered if this calling for me to serve tables is soon to be over. I am a grouchy old man, no doubt and I try not to project it. But after a few days and these comments, I treat everyone like regular customers. I know it sounds stupid to ask someone how they have been lately, if you have never seen them before. I'm trying.

I've been gigged before in email complaints for saying "no" to a guest, which was taken to be rude and curt. No surprise there. When you order something that does not normally come with your meal, you should expect to pay more. When you buy a car and you order Bluetooth or GPS, it's extra. When you order a $6.00 cheese pizza with three topping, it's extra. So when you order a burger with extra cheese and bacon, or an omelet with "egg beaters" or fruit instead of grits, IT'S EXTRA! I don't say no anymore when they make a special request; I just let them know there is a slight up charge. If you don't let them know, they will take it out on; you guessed it, the tip.

I got severely beaten up one day when at 3:30 in the afternoon a lady wanted to know if she could get breakfast. I explained that some things were not available, but I would do my best to accommodate her and her 90 year old Mom. She ordered breakfast for her Mom and she wanted grits, one item I told her was not available after 2:00pm, so she asked what she could have and I told her cottage cheese, fruit or sliced tomatoes.

All of these items are available for a "slight up charge". She ordered fruit and consumed the entire meal and went through the entire payment process all the way to paying the check. After paying with a credit card she complained about the upcharge for the fruit. Really!!! Realizing she was being a Bitch, after she told me she can get the same breakfast somewhere else for less, I doubt it, I'm asking myself the question, why she didn't go there and hopefully she will next time. I reopened her check, deleted the payment, removed the upcharge and reprocessed the credit card payment. That's a lot of work by the way. I re-presented the check so she could leave a tip, but I am not hopeful. You guessed it if you said, 10%. Why I help people I don't know. I should have said "screw it no breakfast after 2:00pm" and hoped she'd never come back.

Everyday I'm asked if it's included and when I say "no" they don't want it. I don't hold much promise for more than a 15% tip from those folks. Stay positive. There are people however, who don't care. They want what they want. They don't care what it cost and they are great tippers. Good Luck.

9

Frugal

Go ahead and sit outside in my patio section. It's 85 degrees and 99% humidity and I not exactly wearing beach attire to wait on you. I am more appropriately dressed to wait on people in the air-conditioned indoor section of the restaurant. You don't have a dog, don't smoke, you didn't just run five miles to get there, and so I don't understand why you're sitting outside. I am on my A Game today and approach the table within 15 seconds. It's an older couple, meaning older than me, and I get the look! You know the look. We've been here for a long while and where in hell have you been look! Swallow that one; pleasant greeting as each customer usually brings a new experience. Remember I told you never judge a book by its cover, you never know.

I take the order which is pretty straight forward, for a change; ring it into the kitchen and Boom, 4 minutes later the food is on the table. There is nothing missing and nothing wrong. Perfect. They happen to catch the kitchen at a lull. I don't know if I told we have the Best Breakfast Chef this side of the Mason Dixon line. The restaurant is only half full and food flies out of the kitchen. I don't know if they were impressed but I was. Usually when the dining experience is that fast, tips are usually pretty good. Not this time!!! I go to collect the check, as I always place the check at breakfast right after the meals are served, as my odds of selling after dinner drinks and dessert at that time of the day are slim to none. He is fumbling with cash and tells me he is not ready to give me the check yet.

I believe he is stuck on calculating the tip. I could offer to help, as I have an uncanny ability to determine what 20% of any number is in my head, but that would be unprofessional. He then watches my movements out of the corner of his eye as I am watching my cash, out of the corner of mine. I then go inside to do what I do in my inside station and they leave. I quickly return to collect my checkbook, as we are self cashiers and responsible for all monies at the end of the day. The check was $20.29. In the checkbook was $22.29. You're Kidding, Right. They left is such a hurry, I did not even get a chance to properly thank them. Their departure time was definitely calculated so I was not there when they left.

I will arrive with a cheerful attitude tomorrow because despite the two bucks, it was actually a good day. The only really bad days are when all of the two buckers sit in your section in the same day. Always remember to recap your week in tips, and not your days or even your tables. It will depress you and you shouldn't worry about it, as there is nothing you can do about it.

At the end of a busy day, a couple arrives and orders two breakfast. One is a special Lox Omelet, which normally comes with Lox, onions, tomato and capers. This guest doesn't want tomato or capers, no problem. I place the order immediately as it's the end of the day and I really want to go have a beer. I had a discussion with the kitchen and we confirmed the guest's request. 10 minutes has passed at this time. 10 minutes later, my table is still not eating. I immediately go to the kitchen to check and the food is gone, (and it is not at the table). Where is it? I give the kitchen the special instructions again and they remake the order, no tomato, and no capers, just Lox, eggs and onions. I go to the table and apologize for the wait, now 20 minutes has passed and I explain that there was a mistake.

They thank me for the update and I get them more coffee. There are very few people in the restaurant as it is very close to closing time, so it must have seemed like a really long wait. The order is now ready and I deliver the food and apologize again. I now check the time on the check to see the elapsed time, as my system has that capability. 34 Minutes. That's from order taking, making and remaking and delivery. I return to the table to check on things and am told they have been there over an hour. It was actually 34 minutes not an hour?

I apologize again and explained it may have felt like a long time but it has only been 34 minutes. EKKKK! Wrong answer I guess. I know no one likes to be told they are wrong or be corrected, but 34 minutes on a Sunday or any day for that fact is still not bad. Now the guest complains that the Chef didn't put any onions in the omelet. I apologize again, anybody counting these apologies for the kitchen, and I delete the omelet from the bill. Want to guess what the tip was. You guessed it if you said Zero. Except for me correcting the exaggerated lie about the time, which I felt was a cheap shot; I don't think I deserved nothing for the effort I put forth.

Never correct a guest. I think if anyone went out and got a meal in 34 minutes, I don't think they would complain. I just get a little tired of people complaining needlessly and trying to get a free meal. Maybe that's what they were looking for. Maybe I should not have kept them up to speed and just told stories to them until their remake arrived. I just don't know sometimes. Although it was not my fault, I suffered the consequences, no tip.

A guy comes in once or twice a week. He seems to be a pretty nice person, friendly and all, but a little demanding. He stays a while, over an hour for breakfast. He requires flavored coffee and several trips to refill his cup. He orders breakfast and wants sliced tomatoes instead of home fries and we tell people it's a slight upcharge (extra cost) as it is not stated on the menu. Last year we didn't charge extra for tomatoes, but in the last year the price has tripled from $9.00 a case to $28.00 a case. The meal is done, the check is paid with a credit card and the guy tells his server, not me, that he is not leaving her a tip. When she asked why, he explained that she charged extra for the sliced tomatoes. Well here is how I look at this. The man ordered something EXTRA, was told it was EXTRA, so we charged him EXTRA. If we pay extra for it, than you pay extra for it. What does her gratuity have to do with price of tomatoes?

I hope this man doesn't get slower service and coffee refills next time he is in, because that would only be fair. Sometimes I wish we knew what kind of tip we were going to get, before we provide our ultimate service. It take all kinds of people to make the world go around, some just make it go a little less profitable for others.

A large party comes in, 6-8 people and dinner is ordered and Dad offers to pay the check. The problem is Dad doesn't realize that 20% is the going rate. He's stuck in rounding up to the nearest $20 dollar bill or a nice round number like $100.00. So if the check is $88 and he rounds to $100, you're screwed. The real problem is that no one argues with him because he is paying the bill. It happens all the time and solutions are far and few between. You can always offer the add 20% to the bill for his convenience, as a great number of people have problems with math calculations. This is actually a service, or you can tell Dad you can leave it up to his good judgment. Some places have a large party policy, but why settle for 20% when it could be more. A roll of the dice I imagine.

It's a thin line between offering to add a tip and insulting the guest. Be careful and if you have established a rapport with the table, different subject, this should not be a problem. I have also seen on many occasions that another person in the party will kick in extra cash as they know Dad is a lousy tipper. I always appreciate that.

I see all kinds of coupons all the time. Some people are really good with this and realize they just saved a bunch of money and tip really well. Some people are just morons when it comes to this. The only way I have figured to combat this is to present the check without the discount. It looks like an honest mistake. This puts a number in the bill payers mind as to what the gratuity should be. Apologize and come back to the table with the corrected amount. A real moron will still leave a gratuity on the discounted amount, but maybe your technique will work. Good Luck.

A single lady had lunch today, paid her check and said "Keep the Change". She also said be careful as there are coins inside. There were ALL coins inside. I guess she really meant keep the change. I wonder where that phrase came from. Can I assume that what is left over is for me? I had a guest leave $25 and said keep the change. The problem was the check was $29. Before I left the table I checked as I always do and I let her know that the check was short. She said she thought the check was $19. How does a two look like a one? I can see a three looking like a five or a one looking like a seven, but not a one looking like a two. Sometimes when people say keep the change and the tip looks like I'm getting screwed, I return the change so you are reminded of how much you are not leaving me.

Open those check presenters before you leave each table to be sure you have a clear understanding of what should be done. Some people still think 10% is a good tip. It happens to me all the time.

Do you think a server deserves a flat rate, $2, $5, $10, $20? Remember we make a flat rate $4.29/hr in my state. The tip should be based on the check, not the time of day, the meal, or anything else. A $20 lunch is a $4.00 tip not $2.00. A $120 dinner is not a $20 tip, it's $24.00. I wonder how people calculate the tip. I had a reporter come in one night and loved everything about the place, a bottle of wine ($10 off special) and four entrees. He told me he was going to write an article in his publication and that the service was great. The check was $107 and the tip was $18 tip, which is not 20%. I don't get it.

A couple comes in once a week and they love me. It's a lot of work, coffee refills decaf and regular, extra napkins and HOT Maple syrup for the pancakes. Hot water refills for the hot tea and iced water requested at three separate times. It's all about special orders and just a lot of attention. They tell me how much they love the place the food and the service. The bill is always $40 and the tip is always $6. Don't get it!

Remember that $18 and $6 a week calculates to $1248 a year. So live with it and accept it because you could always do worse.

Know your name; know your order, lunch served in 12 minutes, $2 on $20. Don't get it!

Older people seem not to tip appropriately. I mean older than me. They seem to tip 10-15%. Don't get it! Very old people, a lot older than me can tip even worse. They have lunch, separate checks, and it's no big deal. They are well off judging by the labels on their clothes and the fact they are dripping with diamonds. Ten percent just seems messed up! Don't get it!

10

Staffing

Come on already! Another personal tragedy has occurred with one of my fellow workers and we are short handed AGAIN! This is really okay with me as I can change gears and make a ton of money, but it's a lot of hard work at my age. It gets old after a while. Wake up folks. Take care of yourselves. You don't work, you don't make money. Tips, remember. If you get sick pay, $4.00 an hour isn't paying the bills. That's if you get sick pay, I don't. There is sick, really sick and, my favorite, The Bottle Flu. This occurs when you don't drink responsibly, know when to say when, and call in with flu like symptoms and call it food poisoning, when you are just still screwed up from the night before. When you do this to me, I have to drag these old bones around at a faster pace than I planned on today. I get pissed at you for a while and if it occurs frequently, you are gone. The turnover in my restaurant is so high, when my Snowbirds return from up north, after 3 months, remember we are in Florida, they don't recognize anyone but me.

You can't party like a rock star anymore. You're getting old. Remember the days when you could drink all night, have sex till dawn and still be at work on time and kick ass to boot. Not anymore cowboys and cowgirls. That's why they invented days off. Get sloshed the night before your day off or at least try to get 6 hours of sleep before your shift. Food poisoning, really!

I've heard, too tired to come to work, picking may car up at the shop and will be late (on a Sunday?). I knew a girl who had 5 flat tires in a month and ran out of gas 4 times in six weeks (same girl). See how many jobs you have had in the last three years and grow up and change that. I haven't missed a day of work in 30 years and yes, I get colds and I drink. So unless I'm in jail for a DUI or in the hospital with a broken bone, I'M AT WORK!!!!

Look around and see who's not really working. In the old days we used to call it "Dogging It", not to be confused with the British term for voyeurism. I work with people all day who really do just what they have to, to make it through the day. Watch people. They walk fast, look busy, hurry from place to place and have the look and verbal sounds of busyness. Huffing and puffing all day while really doing nothing. Looking busy is an art. If you look busy, no one will ask to do anything. If you take a ten minute job and spend an hour doing it, you look busy for an hour. Where I work, there is ALWAYS something to do. If you go to the bathroom several times a day, no one will come looking for you, but if you add it up it could be ½ to one hour a day. Then there are smoke breaks. Six of these per day @ 8 minutes is almost another hour. So now that you have killed almost 3 hours of your 8 hour shift while I am working my conscientious butt off, I really see what is going on. I get annoyed because I have to work harder and faster to get out on time.

Slackers are everywhere. I recently started handing out assignments with the phrase, "before you go home today". I don't care when you get it done, as long as you get it done before you go home. Getting even with slackers in inevitable, because some day, they will be left holding the bag and no one will be there to do the work except them.

Looking for a job in this economy is hard. Sexual harassment, favoritism, unfair schedules, and bad managers often make us want to change jobs. Beware of where to look. The number one rule is to look every day. Search in the local papers, job sites or Craig's List. Don't apply for jobs from places that are constantly looking. There is a reason for that. If a local restaurant is looking and you haven't seen a post in six months, it's telling you they have little turnover, the employees are happy and you probably want to work there. Get your best together and GO FOR IT!

Daily is the key word here. It is also better if you are working, as you get to let the right people know you are looking. Make the effort to fill out those long online applications and hit the internet EVERYDAY. It just takes one day to miss the perfect job for you. Make it your ritual. Good Luck.

Who gets the better station and the better schedule goes back to who gets to wait on Christ at the Last Supper. Schedules should be made out using seniority. If there is some cutting to do, it's longevity that I think is fair. Competency is another factor, as a better server should have a better station and schedule. However, if a person with seniority is less competent than a newer server, then a quandary exists. So what is to be done?

One of my favorite sayings is "You cannot afford not to hire someone, who has more potential than someone who is already on your staff". That being said, who gets the better schedule? I would rather have more competent servers working than more senior servers. If I was running the joint, that makes more sense, wouldn't you? The key is to always hire better servers than what you currently have, that way your level of competency always improves. There actually is no reason to keep an incompetent server just because of longevity. Are you following this?

Look at yourself and evaluate where you stand on the competence ladder. It may require you to "step up" your game so you can rise to the top. I did that last year when I was forced to work with "super woman", and I couldn't keep up with her, sales or tips. I had to dig down deep and step up my game. A little swallowing was involved, a little self evaluation, and a lot of determination. I did it and am so much happier and wealthier for it. I now wish the other people I work with would step up their game. Mo Money!!!

Serving is not for everyone. It requires physical abilities and well as mental skills. You have to be an extremely organized person in order to multi-task constantly for your entire shift. Every second counts. The hiring process is an important one as hiring someone with experience is easy. But what do you look for when hiring someone without experience. One of my first questions is "Have you ever held a job that required you to be at work at 6:00am"? Don't tell me you're a morning person or your uncle owns a breakfast place, just answer the question.

Look for multi tasking experience. I would hire someone who worked in a convenience store in a heartbeat. This individual handles 24 gas pumps, makes coffee all day, does lottery, money orders, takes multiple forms of payment, cash, credit cards, debit cards and gives instructions to the morons who don't know how to use them. They can count $9.82 in coins for gas in 10 seconds. You know the individual I am talking about. They would make a great server. Someone hired a girl for me once who served popcorn and sodas at a movie theater. Training this girl was an intense, comprehensive, elongated project. After finally making a server out of her, she quit and went to work in another restaurant. Thanks for the training!

Next time you are out to eat, observe the skills of your server. They can usually pour coffee from 4 feet away, they can balance 14 things on their tray and not spill a drop and they can handle all your separate checks, cash, making change and process all your credit cards. They ring checks, split checks, order food and make your skim Decaf Cappuccinos. We are pretty talented aren't we?

After work today, there is a cleaning party scheduled, clean till your done! It turned out to be four hours long from 2-6pm. Well, after a full day of work on Sunday, no one is really in the mood for this but, we were given a months' notice. Every six months or so every restaurant needs a DNC (Dusting and Cleaning). Let me paint you a picture. From floor to ceiling, wall to wall and every piece of equipment is moved or disassembled and cleaned. Ten people are scheduled and ten show up and the party begins. Assignments are handed out and directions are given and for about two hours everything is great. Now that the restaurant is torn apart and cleaned, everything needs to be put back together. No one is really interested in the next part as some beer runs were made and everyone is tired, cranky and a little tipsy. Lot of projects are only half done, as the things taken apart now need to be reassembled. I try to motivate them as I am the senior employee, but I have no luck. There is more dancing to loud music, drinking and storytelling being done, as opposed to cleaning and finishing up. I finally make it to the end, a little frustrated and ask if everything is put back together and functional. I get all yeses, but they have no clue. I toss everyone out and someone says "let's go have a drink!" This suggestion is pure genius. Most of us went home. It was a 12 hour day after all.

The next day I arrive @ 6:30am and as I figured, some things are not assembled, some are not plugged in and something is leaking very badly. After looking for nuts, bolts, power cords, and resetting circuit breakers we finally get the place open. Thanks to my forty years of experience, I was able to quickly assess what needs to be done with the knowledge of why and how things in a restaurant work i.e. gas, electricity, water, drainage, etc.. Luckily this only happens twice a year.

The people who work the night shift are definitely cut from a different cloth. I work the day shift and I will try to explain some of the universal differences between the two. We all have timers and most of the day crew I know are like Cheetahs after a prey, zero to 60mph in no time flat. The night crew is more like a school bus on a field trip; it will get to 60mph sometime during the trip but not anytime soon. The day crew, up before sunrise, is ready to go from the start of their day. The night crew takes a while to get going as it takes a while for all the necessary components of the body to wake up. Ask a day crew member to do something and after 5 minutes when you check for an update you hear "what's next'. Ask to same task of the night crew and you get a response like "what did you want?" They will however get it done, but it will probably be before the shift is over. The only real speed you will see from the night crew is at closing time. There is only a set amount of time to consume alcohol between the time they get out and last call. So if anything needs to get done, then this is the time to ask.

Remember what the pace of the night crew is. If you need them to work a day shift, schedule them 1 hour earlier than you need them to perform, so they can wake up. Some people are just day crew and some are just night crew. Very rarely does a night crew successfully transform into a day crew, although I have seen it happen. Also remember that if something is not done or is done incorrectly for the next day, the day crew will always blame the night crew.

Hiring the right people is a difficult task. Testing is good but you cannot get the real skill level of your potential new hire by written testing. Asking a chef to name the 5 mother sauces or a server to name Champagne from California, is just a measure of hospitality IQ. If you really want to see what your new potential employee can do, take them to a live work station. Then ask them to show you their stuff. Ask the bartender to pour ten shots in drink glasses and then measure them to see if the bartender can pour a measured shot. Ask them to make you a Mojito. Ask them to pour you two draft beers. Ask your chef to make you three over light eggs one in each pan. Then ask him or her to dice a bell pepper in a quarter inch dice. Ask you servers to clear a four top of entrée plates stacking them on one arm only. Then set up 5 coffee cups in the middle of a 36" table. Place one cup in the center and the other four around it in a circle. Ask the server to pour coffee in the center cup without picking it up using only one hand.

This enables you to watch the person work and it cuts through all the bullshit people are sometimes good with during the interview. So if you want a bartender who knows how to move and pour an accurate shot and doesn't waste half of your draft beer, you found your person. If you want a cook who knows how to use a knife, follow instructions and is not going to fill a trash can with a bunch of broken eggs, then you found you person. If you want a server that is coordinated, can think on their feet and actually has experience, you found your person. We have all hired to wrong person at one time or another before. If you perform a background check, do a drug test, check references, and have a great interview, I don't think that it's near enough. It's your place and you have every right to test the way you want. Good luck.

II

Service

Good money is yielded from good service. If you don't give the best service you don't make major bucks. You can make a real decent living at this if you do it right.

Let's start with your game face. Show up every day in a great mood or better. Show that game face when you approach your tables. It shows them that you are in charge, you are a professional, and ready to make money. Next you have to know your stuff. You need to know your menu, all the capabilities of the kitchen as well as your own. Be sure what you promise the guests, you can deliver. If you don't you will be the one to suffer. Be the fastest person in the house on your POS (computer system). I used to study the different screens and go to screens I hadn't been to before. I always look for short cuts. The less time you spend at the computer the more time you can spend doing other things or spending time with your guests. It is true that the more time you spend with your guests the higher the percentage of tips will be. That is why you make good money on a slow day because your percentage is higher.

Set you mind straight every day. You need to get ahead of the game every day and stay there. Sometimes I just pretend to be slammed at noon everyday even if I am not. It's psychological. Then if I get crushed I am already in attack mode. Try it.

Another way to make great money and provide perceived great service is to let people think you are doing something special just for them. It could be a special exception or a special order or even something that is not on the menu. It's no big deal we know but the perception goes on for miles and usually turns out higher tips. The next key is to be a team player all the time. I have left an empty station many times to take a break and upon returning, the entire station fills up all at once. It happens all the time. If you are a team player all the time only your fellow employees can rescue you from this dilemma. However if they remembered that you seldom or never help them they will just watch you drown. It's only fair.

Organization is the key to success in this industry. After your meals are down, put your checks down. Do as many as you can at one time too. It saves time. People like to pay at their convenience and should not have to wait for checks. Hey if someone orders something else like dessert, you can always reprint the check. This way your people are in and out. Bus your own table if you have to. If you want to have a discussion about whose job that is, then I will have a new party and you will still be looking for your busser. Higher turnover again means more money. I call it "Turn and Burn".

Use names whenever you can. If you know them use their names as people love to hear the sound of their own name. Say it with diction and a little higher volume. People love that. If you don't know it then steal it off the credit card if they use one. Then when you return to the table you can say "have a great weekend Mr. Jones". I'm sure he will wonder how the hell you knew his name. Then he will figure out that you are pretty sharp.

Look at your game and figure out ways to improve it. If you can't figure it out on your own, then try watching your fellow employees to see what they do. You should always be looking for ways to improve your game. For breakfast I set up remote satellite stations for coffee and extra creamers to save time. For lunch I set up iced water and iced tea refill pictures. Put condiments on each table. I put less ice in my soft beverages to eliminate returning for refills. Do anything you can think of to save time which will increase your speed and efficiency.

All these goodies that you learn and do for yourself help you save time and make more money. Do the math. If you spend 2 extra minutes at each table and you wait on 30 tables every day, you save an hour in loss productivity. It's all about making money and getting out as early as you can. No one wants to hang around for $4 an hour if you're not making any tips.

Bartending is a not only a job, it's an art and a lifestyle. If you have never tended bar than you probably have no idea how difficult and fun it is at the same time. It requires skills, coordination, knowledge and a great personality. First are the skills. You need to be fast, efficient, accurate at not only making the drinks, but performing cash register transactions. This includes ringing up checks, running tabs, credit cards and making change for cash customers. Second is coordination. You need to have great hand-eye coordination as your movements are various, your speed needs to be incredible and you need to be able to move in a way that gets you around all night. If you're working with others, you need to know how to stay out of their way. It's like having great sex with a great partner. Third is the knowledge of all that liquor. There is the difference between sour mash and bourbon or the difference between a cordial and an aperitif. It also requires the knowledge of all those drinks. That includes all the oldies like Sidecars and

Presbyterians and all the new ones like Sex on the Beach, Blow Jobs, and Screaming Orgasms; just to name a few. Last is a great personality. You need to be able to handle stress and have your best money making game face on all the time. Being in the weeds and greeting a guest like you are so happy to see them is an art.

Wine service is becoming a lost art. I am not sure what to do anymore as the days of first growth wines and where Champagne comes from are all but long gone. The ritual of wine service should be learned and remembered. Present the wine, open and present the cork to the host and offer a taste below the spring line, serve the remaining guest, finishing with the host. We all know that, right? But my question is what do I do with the twist off aluminum cap? Times have changed and if Robert Mondavi knew then what we know now, he wouldn't have spent all that money on corks.

I used to save bottles and corks from the service bar and recork empty bottles to have the staff practice opening wine in menu class (pre-meal training classes). I had an issue with some of the staff not knowing how to open wine or felt uncomfortable opening it in front of guests. Henceforth I held training classes. I had a server that used to pay a fellow server $5 to open wine for her. A little training and the problem was solved. Personally I used to use an Osso to pull my corks, a lost art, but some of the newer methods of making corks (plastic) make me lose the cork in the process. I have resorted back to the traditional wine key. Wine is a big deal when it comes to check average, so knowledge and comfort play a huge role in your income. Don't be afraid to sell bottles.

If you don't know the ritual, learn it. For those who know it, have fun with the twist off cap. A true wine lover will know what you are doing and enjoy the fact that you know "how it's done".

12

Workaholic

Work smarter not harder. That's the key to successful management. A workaholic is defined as somebody addicted to work: somebody who has a compulsive need to work hard and for very long hours. It is also defined as someone who spends most of their time working and has little interest in other things. That is no way to live your life. Dedication is a rare quality to find in people today. It does not mean you need to spend your life at work. Arriving at work early and staying late proves nothing. After a while your fellow employees will just think you're nuts.

There are people who are so connected to work that they become compulsive. They check their cell phones every ten minutes for messages or emails. They are glued to their Blackberries; their PC's and brings work home with them. This tells me that you are not very organized or your boss is a workaholic and thinks everyone in the rest of the world needs to be also. I had a boss once who would call me at five o'clock in the evening and ask where I was. When I told him I was home he appeared shocked that I was home at such an early hour. Well after arriving at six in the morning, I consider an eleven hour day enough.

You need to set up your own rules and stick by them religiously. I opened a 2000 room hotel and it was a nightmare as most openings can be. Long hours are expected as the mountain of work that needs to be accomplished is enormous. It's all about meeting the Grand Opening date. It's understandable. After you get open however it's a different story. I was in purchasing for food and beverage. I was responsible for $9m a year in goods. It's a lot of stuff if you can only imagine. So I set up rules. All deliveries were between the hours of 8:00am and Noon. Trucks that showed up after noon were turned away. All the salespeople and companies I dealt with knew the rules. Requisitions were filled to the 11 restaurants and 14 bars between during that time as well. Between the hours of noon and 2:00pm nothing was done. My staff took lunch, and I took lunch. Everyone needs a break during the day. There was always a lot of stress at this property as it was the company's new baby. All eyes were on the Bismarck. Located in Manhattan, the pace was always incredible. There were constant new demands it seemed daily and everything needed to be done now not later. It's just the way New York City is. Between noon and two was when I ate a little something and got most of my work done. Everyone was at lunch and the two storerooms were closed everyday for those two hours. It was a very productive. After 2:00pm all the orders were placed for the day. While management was placing orders the rest of the staff were putting away the morning's deliveries. Food orders were placed by teletype (1985) and liquor, beer, and wine were ordered by phone. If a salesperson called before two, they were dismissed. I also never allowed salespeople to visit. No one has time for that chit chat. It's just a bunch of bullshit. By the time 4:30 rolled around everything was done and most of the time everyone went home on time.

There was however my wonderful peers in operations who would stay on into the night as some of them were workaholics and most of them were just unorganized. At this hotel, it's probably the only 8-5 job I ever had and I loved my little system. Remember never deviate.

In everything you do you need to set up a system. Do things daily for 5 minutes instead of doing the big chore weekly for 35 minutes. Doing things like calculating food cost, beverage cost and doing inventory are time consuming enough in themselves. You can either figure out a way to be more efficient or spend your life at work. Two things you can do are delegate or automate. I worked for a guy once who held on to the apron strings so tight, he wouldn't let me do important tasks. He wanted to do everything himself to make sure it was right. The problem is you become indispensible and no one underneath you ever learns or grows. Cut those strings and spread the work load around. Motivate and train your subordinates to do some of your work for you. They will have to learn it sometime. It might as well be now. Go out or go home and enjoy life before it passes you by.

Automation was and still is my best friend. At the end of every fiscal period there is all the closing stuff that needs to be done. It's just the corporate way. You can't get away from it so figure out a better way to deal with it. I would write simple spreadsheet programs to calculate inventories, month end results, and costs of sales. All these were previously done by hand. It was estimated to perform all these duties about 60 hours of calculator time. I got it down to just a few hours. So while I was out playing golf on a Saturday, my peers were stuck on calculators looking at spreads sheets for a day and a half with their assistances. I will admit I spent hundreds of hours (no exaggeration) developing these programs but in the end it was more than worth the quality of life I enjoyed while others just looked like workaholics.

Work smarter not harder or longer. That is my message. When I commuted to the city every day, I would take two hours of work with me every night. I would do one hour on the way home and the other hour on the way into work. I never worked in my home as that's a big no no. I did it on the train. I was just being productive as there isn't much to do on a train. I worked for a major hotel company who had a standard work week philosophy. You should work 50 hours per week, 10 hours a day, five days a week. They used to say that if you couldn't get it done in 50 hours, then you were doing something wrong.

Owning your own business will definitely make you a workaholic. Hey it's your money were talking about not some major corporation. I operated a New York style Delicatessen in Florida for three years. Days off were few and vacations were a thing of the past. My pay consisted of what was left over every week. Some weeks were better than others. The harder you work the more money you make. There was no salary. It was seven days a week for the first year and then six days after that. If you have a certain sense of pride to get things done right, you have to almost do everything yourself. So I worked my butt off every day for three years to be successful.

Would I do it again? I wouldn't work that hard again but I would entertain the thought of opening another restaurant. I guess we just have more energy when we are younger.

Working as a Maitre D' in a 400 room hotel, some genius booked a group of kids (high school seniors) for three days. There were 900 of them. The booked them two to three to a room and we tried to capture them for their meals. Being out our league size wise, we had to go above and beyond the call of duty to feed these kids for three days. We created pizza bars and deli stations as well as the normal restaurants. Everything was buffet style as the group was too large to offer menu service. So I worked 76 hours in a row. After every meal we would set up for the next meal. I slept maybe two hours a night in my office and then back at it again.

After the third day of serving thousands of meals, the General Manager threw us out of the hotel. He said I don't want to see you guys for the next two days. Most of those two days were spent sleeping, trust me.

Most major corporations evaluate their financial performance monthly. In food and beverage, inventories are performed and costs are calculated to provide accurate P&L statements. In the newest of hotels they established a goal of a daily P&L at this property. I am hired on to achieve this goal as I am considered to be the best at writing programs for this kind of thing. It is the mid-eighties and the PC is a new thing to everyone. I am using program versions using the number one. Programs like Word Perfect 1.0 and Lotus 1.0 were all that there was back then. I wrote on 5" floppy disks using more than one disk on occasion to accommodate the data. My daily cost program used 7 disks to calculate the daily liquor, beer, and wine cost for 14 bars and restaurants. The estimated calculation to crunch these numbers manually was 24 hours per day or three employees. I worked tirelessly on a theoretical program for 400 hours to get it right. That would be 10 weeks at 40 hours per week. However I only had 6 weeks until opening. Not to mention I other stuff to do.

You can definitely call me a workaholic but the work had to get done. They were paying me a handsome salary to do this as well. As a result of my efforts and genius my goal was accomplished and the daily calculations including printing the reports on a Dot Matrix printer took a total of only 53 minutes. Not bad Huh?

Working overnight and sleeping on ten cases of beer in a storeroom is certainly a workaholic. It's the first closing period of a major hotel and there is an insurmountable amount of work to do. This had never been done before on such a scale. There was only one solution, work through the night. So with the assistance of lots of coffee and adrenaline, I processed paperwork all night. Only grabbing 2 hours of sleep from 4:00am to 6:00am, I finish the intended task by the require time of noon.

Henceforth the following closings were less time consuming as we learn from our own experiences that I am not going to do this every month.

Throughout your entire career, try to be consistent. Be real and extremely organized. If everyone knows that you are not wishy washy, then you will be respected. Be a no-nonsense type of manager and you will go far.

13

Catering

Every off property catering gig is an adventure in itself, as you never know what to expect. You don't know the people, the equipment, the lay out (1st floor, penthouse, elevators, ramps, etc.). You also have to have an extensive checklist to remember everything, as you will be away from your home base and will not be able to return if you forget something. Last night starts out with the entire crew and all the food in the same vehicle and it breaks down 1/3 of the way there, great! Now a series of phone calls are made to try to get us to the location on time. We succeed and arrive late, but in enough time to pull it off. The kitchen is crowded with a slew of people and there is no room to work. This is actually pretty typical as most hostesses don't trust the cooking skills of the caterer. We were hired to provide hors d'oeurves only. Now we are setting up a bar and preparing food that is not ours. There is of course no mention of this in the contract. We comply; as that is what we do, go above and beyond the call of duty, only to get criticized for it, at the end. You can never do enough for people. Hired to provide hors D'oeurves, we prepare their food, store it (in their Zip-Lock bags), wash their dishes, make their coffee, clean their coffee machines, and clean up their bar and kitchen which we were not contracted to use. What a night!

The next event will most likely be the same as the variables are endless. We will be asked to do the impossible, perform the impossible, not get paid for the impossible and probably get criticized for the impossible. It's still good money and that's why we will continue to do, the impossible!!

Tonight was another exciting off property catering event. Two Jewish girls are coming of age and a Bar Mitzvah for 160 people. As I said in an earlier blog, off property is a new experience each and everytime. Someone always forgets something. It was a nice party actually. There was an open bar, beer and wine, buffet dinner with an ice cream bar and a DJ with lots of dancing. We only forgot a few things this time like plastic cups for lemonade and iced tea, napkins and a beer run needed to be made as you never can guess what people will drink. That was not bad over all. Going to the store in the middle of an event is just such a hassle. You have to break someone out of the mix, find some cash, making a list, and give directions to the nearest store. It's the little things that we always forget like the cream for the coffee or the butter for the dinner rolls. You know the things you HAVE to have. I worked with a bunch of complete strangers as I was called in off the bench for this one at the last minute. Nice people all of them and even the guests were nice. It was just a pleasant evening all around. There was a maintenance man in attendance, just to make sure we behaved. His big thing was recycling. This is something we don't do at any of the three stores I work at. It was a little challenging getting use to something new, but we made it work.

Up before dawn and back to the grind I go. High season has passed and most of us are a little cranky as sales, hours and tips are down, not to mention the "Road Closed "sign, in front of my location. The county is doing some work for five weeks. So the road is closed and I will suffer (financially) for 5 weeks.

As Tropical Storm Debby pounds Florida for four days, we are on the beach catering a wedding. Upon arrival we discover a tent where this event is to happen located 150 feet from the kitchen, which is equipped with an oven a little bigger than a Betty Crocker Easy-Bake oven. We unload and start setting up the bar and the buffet table. Moving back and forth from vehicles to the Tiki bar and the tent, it only takes seconds to become drenched. Adjusting to circumstances as we do at catered events, we are sharing the tiny Tiki bar with the DJ. The bar has now become the hor's d'oeurves table and the coffee station. The bride, groom, wedding party, some really good friends and the "Internet Minister", all carrying umbrellas, head to the beach as the ceremony begins. All goes really well except for the pounding rain. It was a really nice group of people, only 45 in all. One guest commented that the Spanikopia was supposed to be served crisp. I don't know how anything could be crisp, served outside in the middle of a tropical storm. Someone's unsupervised child decides it would be cool the feed the Seagulls. Now, in the middle of dinner, it looks like a scene from the Alfred Hitchcock movie "The Birds" as Seagulls are swooping around the tent for food.

There is an old wives tale that says if it rains on your wedding day it means money is in your future. This couple will be filthy rich. Throughout the night I am having flashbacks about snuggling with a gorgeous redhead, a blazing log in the fireplace, and drinking a real good bottle of French Bordeaux.

After flopping around in the rain for 7 hours, like a duck on a pond, at the tail end of my 18 hour day, (worked my breakfast lunch shift earlier), we head home. A few things are now in order. We will start with a hot shower and some dry clothes. Next would be a trip to the drug store to get some Zinc to prevent getting Pneumonia, some rest and a least a good glass of Pinot Noir.

After the holiday weekend is over and 48 hours are worked in four days, it's time to share Sunday's catering gig with you. Dinner is scheduled for 65 people in a huge house. As off-property catering always holds lots of surprises, this dinner was on the pool deck. If the pool deck can feed 65 for a sit down dinner, you can only imagine the size of the rest of the house. If I get lost inside the house looking for the garage, then the house is too big. Moving all the pool furniture is required to be replaced with rental tables and chairs. All this is performed while wearing a tux, without the jacket, and in 95 ° heat. Other than getting the wrong address, the wrong directions and showing up late, it was a pretty good event.

Finding myself in a parking lot on a hot July day, dressed in a tuxedo and I am asking myself why I am here. We are doing a reception for 300 people for a realtor. It starts with a one hour ride in our truck. After we arrive we are given instructions by the meticulous hostess. This woman was a huge success but I didn't know how her staff put up with her. She expected the impossible. We constructed two bars and four food station in the parking lot with no shade relief from the Florida heat. She makes me park the truck out of sight some 100 feet away from the main area. It is only a problem because we cook on the back of the truck. So it's a little longer walk but we are starting to understand this woman. We just do what were told and shut up. Now she wants all the garbage cans lined with fine linen so no one can tell they are trash cans. Next she wants us to move the breakdown station (for dishes) out of sight as well. Of course we comply. It was a lot of work for what turned out not to be a lot of money. We are paid a gratuity not an hourly pay. What was supposed to be a two hour reception took us with travel time over six hours. This whole event would have been much better if we were all wearing Khaki shorts and Hawaiian shirts. Oh well.

A beach wedding is planned and I am in charge as we load up the truck, give directions to the staff and head to one of Florida's keys. Upon arrival the tent is already set and all the rental equipment has been dropped off by the rental company. So we hustle in the heat, trudging our stuff across the sand and we are about ready to set up the food. While unpacking I notice my coffee percolator is missing the inside basket. You know the part that holds the COFFEE! Now I'm screwed. I call the rental company which was a challenge in itself as cell reception out where we were was iffy at best. So after dropping a bunch of calls I convince the rental company to drive back out to the key in traffic, on a weekend, to give me the ability to make coffee. This was a big mistake on their part.

The wedding goes off without a hitch and we are packing up and someone asks about the chairs on the beach. I say "what chairs?" The rental company had placed 100 chairs on the beach prior to our arrival and now someone has to bring them off the beach into a storage area. It's late and I can't call the rental company so I am screwed. I now have to beg my exhausted staff to pull these chairs some 200 feet off the beach. Like I said catering always holds some unexpected surprises.

Always be mentally prepared to handle the unexpected and do the impossible. That's the excitement of off-property catering and there is always a ton of money to be made.

14

Management

A lot of people do not like their bosses and that is understandable. They control a lot of your life. They schedule unfairly, make demands that seem unreasonable, ride you needlessly, schedule you to work shifts you don't want to work, like holidays, etc. etc. There are some good bosses out there, but it really wouldn't be any fun talking about them now would it. Let's talk about the assholes. In the bad manager categories I will discuss four.

One: KNOWLEDGE AND NO TACT;

This manager has all kinds of knowledge and experience. I mean they know almost everything and you can tell everytime you talk to them. You are impressed. Somewhere along the line, they forgot how to treat people, like you. There is never a request, always a demand, no please or thank-you, and never a when you get time or a minute. Everything is now and there is never a discussion, just do it.

Two: KNOWLEDGE AND NO ACTION;

This manager has all kinds of knowledge and experience. They just never act on anything or do anything. Usually always on vacation, taking the day off, don't have time or will get to it when they can. Things with this type of manager usually take forever to get done, including desperately needed supplies, POS upgrades, payroll issues, and anything that you deem important.

Three: NO KNOWLEDGE AND PLENTY OF EGO;

This manager has little or no experience. Their ego prevents them from learning, being corrected or criticized, and hence they never grow. They have usually had lots of jobs, and lots of untrue excuses to why they were terminated, (oh I'm sorry, they quit). They typically were hired because they know someone or they are real good with bullshit at the interview. Not to worry about this one. They will probably go away soon. This manager should just be ignored except when it comes to job security.

Four: NO KNOWLEDGE AND NO EXPERIENCE;

This person is just out of school with a Degree! Impressed, I'm not. They are fresh out of school and never worked a day in their life, because Daddy put him through school and sent him a healthy allowance so he or she didn't have to work part or full time for spending money. So they have no experience. They still think that weekends are for the beach, boating and barbeques. Wrong! They still think nights are for going out with friends instead of working dinner shifts. So this individual doesn't want to be there at all. Breakfast is too early and nights are too late so lunch is just fine. This one won't be around long either unless he is the owner's niece or nephew.

Remember why we are here. We are here to make money. We have many obstacles and management is one of them. So just deal with it. Managers come and go and you may or may not. My situation is perfect as I am in the fifth management situation, Absentee Management. This is perfect as I am in charge and I am the best boss I know. I have knowledge, experience and have seen everything from the Last Supper to the loading of Noah's Ark.

Bullies don't go away after you get out of school. It's a trait. I won't call it a quality, as in some people, after they demean you, they feel better. This happens way too frequently where I work and I'm sure I am not alone. Imagine getting up at 5:30am, getting pumped up, have a few cups of coffee and feel like you can take on the world. Then, you get to work. Someone asks if you feel alright as you don't look right today. Gee thanks, I feel great. Then your day starts and you get swamped. No problem, you change gears and get it done. Throughout the next few hours of just being spectacular, it starts. The chef has everything to say about every ticket you ring. This is wrong, that is wrong and you need to charge the guest 50¢ for that. It doesn't stop. It just goes on all day. "Your friends" or coworkers can't help because they are slammed as well. The owner walks in, looks around and can't find anything to do so he departs. Customers continue to flock in and there is no light at the end of any tunnel. Just keep pushing; you can do this like you've done a million times before.

There are however good managers out there. Management is defined by "controlling events". They make things happen every minute of every day. It's hard to find good managers these days as things always get in the way. There are the family operations that are screwed up because their blood is thicker than your water. There are partnerships. That means there are usually too many different versions of the right way to do stuff. There is politics which involves power struggles and pure nonsense.

I lost a really good job once because I expected people to be at work on time every day. They called it a hostile work environment. Imagine that, coming to work when you are supposed to. I had the highest profit margin in the company (140 hotels), and a boss from the seventies who didn't care about the employees or me. He just had a ruthless "get it done" attitude. So they let ME go. I learned a long time ago that there are two reasons for your existence as a manager, customer satisfaction and profit. If you have noticed making your employees happy was not one of them. Good luck working for a great manager but remember they are out there.

15

Philosophies

Let's look at how you determine what makes a good day and what makes a bad day. I wonder if it's one thing or it's a combination of things. Remember, the crapiest day can always be classified as a good day if you make big bucks.

Money is always number one for most of us. Some days are just great and there are the days where you can't find a 20% tip. Those are the days you wished you called in sick. Aggravation is next on my measuring stick. Do you have days where you drop a bunch of stuff, let the coffee urn overflow, Chef on your ass all day, and feel totally uncoordinated all day? Or are you "in the zone" and feel like a "Man on Fire" and nothing can stop you? Does your boss affect your day? Does the boss's absence or presence make a difference in your day? Do you have those days where the work load is non-stop from open to close or do you have days where there isn't much to do? Does who you work with, matter to you. I have preferences and I'm sure you do too. Can the type and quality of customers make or break your day? Does volume have an effect on your day? Some days you can't get enough and some days, you wish it would just stop and you really don't care if you make any money. This is when you start cringing when people sit in your station. This is usually followed by the question, "Can I go home early?"

There are a lot of factors that contribute to how you day turns out. It would be super to make great money, have a boss who was great, the best co-workers, and the nicest guests. I doubt there is a perfect combination and I am sure we would all like to find it. If you know where it is, please let me know. So the next time you get stuck opening by yourself because your partner has some lame-ass excuse for being late, you get crushed early because you are not ready, make mistakes all day, get reamed by the Chef, every other ticket, make 15% for the day and have to work late for a different lame-ass excuse, remember, some days are just better than others.

Have you ever had one of those days where you just didn't want to be there? It's the day before Easter and no one is here, so to speak. We are closed on Easter Sunday and everyone has an attitude. I have, hung over and really want to go home. I have hung over and don't want to come to work and I have just don't feel like being here. We all have days like these. You are in love (lust) and you just spend the day wishing you were somewhere else, texting your new lust all day in the bathroom or the parking lot and can't wait to get out. You and I have worked many hours this week and made a ton of money and don't (financially) want to be here. Tomorrow is a holiday and I am already in tomorrow and am no use to the operation today. What a quandary. Nothing is getting done and the day just sucks for me who wants to be here and wants to make some money.

Monday will be better as the holiday will be over and the economy will still suck and I will still have to kiss ass to make a living and everything should go back to normal.

Asking someone to do something these days is just not that simple anymore. I guess there used to be one way to do things, at one time, but that was a long time ago. Today it is different. It you want it done right, you have to spell it out. In the catering department you need to ask these types of questions. What is the start time, the time the staff starts or the time guests arrive and the event starts. For a platter, is it 20 sandwiches, 10 sandwiches cut in half, or 20 sandwiches cut in half? Whenever booking a contract for catering, you must clearly define "clean-up". I know I will clean up my mess, but it cost extra to clean up yours. For scheduling, does the hour on the schedule for the start time indicate a target that you would like me to achieve or is the time you want me dressed, fed and ready to work? Finally, if you have a question, ask it.

Be specific when making requests, (sounds better than making demands). If you want it done a certain way, communicate that to me. If you want me to use my talent, then tell me your objective so we can both obtain the same goal. Please, please don't assume or let me try to read your mind. That never ends up pretty.

Most people are genuinely honest. There is however a certain percentage of people that look to take advantage of every unfortunate mishap. In my business, there are credit cards, IPads, sunglasses, eyeglasses, cameras, iPods and the like left behind every day. In my time there have been things stolen by my fellow employees. In the outside world, when someone finds something that does not belong to them, one of two reactions occurs. Do the right thing, or they think, how I can benefit from this persons mishap. I had my wallet stolen from my vehicle late one night while it was parked in my driveway. They went and got gas but by the time I reported it they were done (all the credit cards were cancelled) and they dumped the wallet. A person who did the right thing, called me to retrieve my wallet. The ID was still intact as it is a PIA (Pain in the Ass) to replace those things. Replacing credit cards is just as bad. I left a cell phone in a shopping cart many years ago when they didn't fit on your belt or in your pocket. A lady called me _five_ days later and said she had found my phone and wished to return it. We made arrangements to meet and she wanted a reward for finding the phone. I thanked her for returning the phone, told her it was a corporate phone and I had it replaced 3 days ago. I tossed the phone in the trash and walked away. A friend of mine lost his credit card this week. Someone found it and flipped the card over and called the credit card company to report it so it could be deactivated. That's doing the right thing.

I know people who have been caught in the act of trying to benefit from someone's mishap. They are still doing time. It's how they think. If you are a good hearted hard working person, with good scruples, you do the right thing. If you are the other type of person, always looking to take advantage of peoples misfortunes, government programs, i.e. food stamps, welfare, etc., some day we all hope you will get what is coming to you. However you can change. The next time you run across something that you find to be left behind and it's not yours, DO THE RIGHT THING. I can cite several examples of people, who have not done it and got busted, ask Bernie Madoff. Hey. Clean up your act and DO THE RIGHT THING, next time, you'll feel better trust me.

The customer is always right, Right? This is not only a philosophy in the service industry, but is not true. It's like the saying, "All things are created equal". They are not. We all know that. Look around your workplace and you know that it is impossible for all things to be created equal. Well, the customer is not always right; I like to let them think they are right. If you don't, they will take it out of your pocket when it comes time to leave the tip. Some examples would be; I said I wanted 3 eggs, not 2 eggs. You actually didn't say that but you were thinking it all morning and you just forgot to tell me. Today a woman sent back a sandwich because the bread was not toasted. I toasted her some new bread and when I redelivered the sandwich, I politely explained to her that all our sandwiches are made not toasted, unless requested otherwise. She said she told me toasted. Did Not!! You are supposed to repeat orders back to people to make sure they are right, but that gets a little redundant after 40 years. So it really is my fault. It's not a big deal, a piece of bread and an extra egg. But when it gets to "I told you egg whites in my omelet and you forgot", and now I am throwing the old one out and making you a new one, and to boot, you are making everyone at the table wait for your remake (your fault) before they can eat. Now everything is cold and I get S**t for a tip. What a wonderful life.

Its' always going to be my fault so I admit it every day to the customers, the waitstaff and the chefs. It's just easier when you tell someone you screwed up, be a man and fess up. That way, no one really can say much. Something tomorrow will be my fault and I will admit it, apologize and then just laugh about it later in the day.

Let's talk about the differences between the average worker and the server, especially me. I make $4.65 an hour plus tips and let's just keep that in mind.

I'm up at 5:30am everyday and you are not up until 7:00am unless you are a health freak and run a large circle every morning for your health.

By 7:30 I have set up a 110 seat restaurant, trayed pastries, made all your favorite beverages, 3 different coffees, portioned cream cheese for your bagels and condiments for you oatmeal. You are not even at work yet.

I kiss ass all morning with special request like Soy milk, 2% milk for coffee, hot decafe teas, no foam lattés, and hot chocolates with whipped cream. You have just read your email, looked out the window and caught some water cooler bullshit.

I consume breakfast standing up, without sitting and grabbing bites when I can. You are probably eating a Danish and drinking coffee while trying to figure out how to earn your salary today.

9:00 Am. Most days I am usually putting together a lunch delivery that I am not getting paid for, again $4.65 an hour. You are definitely having a personal phone call on company time.

All day I perform kitchen functions like prepping sauces, fruit, filling coolers with stock and setting up for lunch. By now its 10:00am and you have made 4 phone calls and returned all of your 6 emails.

Lunch comes and while you are figuring out where to go, who will pay and how you can only leave the waiter a 15% tip, while in a rush. I am dealing with your short schedule and special request and your need for beverage refills like you went out and partied all night. I am running my ass off at full speed while trying to nosh on a cold breakfast mistake in the kitchen.

Lunch is over, it's 2:00pm and my day is almost over and you have 3 hours to go. Now it is time for me to restock. I cut more fruit and prep more stuff for tomorrow. I must now make a trip to the storeroom for supplies. This storeroom is located 400 feet across the main drag as the landlord gives us free space when available so we take what we can get. I get beer to stock for the night shift and vegetables for the cooks and paper supplies for the upcoming shift. Remember $4.65 an hour and not making any tips at this point. You are trying to figure out how to look busy for the rest of your day.

Its 3:00 and I am at the bar with friends enjoying two for one beers (BOGO) and you are finally getting some work done.

I will be up at 5:30am again regardless of all the BMC (bitching, moaning and complaining), and I do it all again. My sidework saves the boss a lot of money and as he describes all my extra duties as, I make good money overall. You have to learn to take the good with the bad. It's hard to find a different job in this economy, so you have to accept it and figure out a way to live with it.

Someone always comes up the great idea of going out for drinks after work which, in forty years, I have found is never a good idea. I am a fan of Happy Hour with a maximum attendance of three! There are some good stories that are told and some form of relaxation, but there is also some danger lurking in the late evening hours. There are statements made that are misunderstood, promises made that will not be remembered or kept and comments made that were not meant to be said. Alcohol impairs judgment. So go to the party. Speak little, drink little, and to avoid a DUI, leave early.

The next day things will be fuzzy. Some regrets may occur, but remember, the less you say, the less you can be quoted on.

Let's talk about sexual harassment for a minute. It puzzles me how stupid management can be at times. There are two aspects of our life. One is work and the other is personal. What is so hard about that? You don't mix gasoline with lit matches, so where is the problem. Hey everyone wants to get laid. There are plenty of customers to pick up or there is always the bar after work or the all-night diners. My recent stories would be four.

First, would be the Sous Chef who took out his muddler in the walk-in in front of a waitress. Was he really expecting her to say "it's about time; I've waited a long time to see that".

Second, would be the owner that offered a waitress some serious money if she would perform services for some regular guests, investors, and suggested it would be in the best interest of her long time employment.

Third would be an owner who was sleeping with a server and her interpretation was, that she could be late, call out, break all of what few rules there were and drink at work (in front of fellow employees) and get away with it. That didn't last but 6 months. Five months longer than it should have.

Forth would have to be all the attention I get from servers of the opposite sex, who only flirt with me and make inappropriate suggestions to me, because I am the guy who makes out the schedule. That's not going to work. I know the separation.

Read the law. It states that you can't do anything that makes anyone feel uncomfortable in the workplace. This includes showing your unit to a staff member in the walk-in, limiting their access or putting them in an uncomfortable situation (restricting egress), telling an off-color or sexually orientated joke or implying sexual favors for mutual gain, or making racial or religious remarks. If you have any questions, you can always look them up under state or federal laws. Come on guys and gals, there is plenty out there and it is always smarter not to dip you pen in the company inkwell.

There are two types of people in this world, Theory X and Theory Y, according to a book written Douglas McGregor. Theory X does just what they need to do to get by. Theory

Y always goes above and beyond the call of duty, and does whatever is necessary for the TEAM. They will get drinks or take orders for guests not in your station because one of your teammates is tied up. They will run food that is not yours and you will do anything the chefs need. Why you do this is, because it comes back to you two fold, at least. When you get jammed up, the chefs will help you and your Theory Y teammates will help you out. It's a pretty situation that you put yourself in and all it requires is EFFORT.

Look at who you want to be, an "X" or a "Y". I like working with "Y's" and I hate working with "X's". Know where to be when, is a form of intuition. If your priorities are screwed up, you probably won't succeed as well as you would like to. Look around and evaluate who's who.

16

Profit

After having lunch today in a new restaurant, I thought I would share my professional opinion with you. I arrived about 11:30am and the place was virtually empty. I was the second table and the counter was empty. Throughout my 90 minute stay, there were only six tables for lunch. When I had a restaurant in a strip mall setting, I would always feed employees from neighboring stores every day. They basically paid my rent. This was not the case. I ordered lunch and it was probably 30 minutes to grill a Reuben in an empty restaurant. A choice of soup or salad was included with the meal. I had soup. It was hot and tasty. The plate was accompanied by more French Fries than the two of us could eat and three pickle spears. The sandwich was very good and I was stuffed afterwards not realizing a choice of dessert is also included. I ordered the Peach Cobbler. Fifteen minutes later the cobbler arrives as it had to be heated. I took a bite or two but really had no room left in my stomach. The meal was $6.95 and the service was great. With three servers on duty, I expected no less. I paid the bill, left the usual overtip and continued on with my day.

We hear every day in the news about how people come into a company and shake things up. This needs to be done here. The definition of management is "to control events". If you have no business, first, you need to find out why. Hand out flyers, advertise, do something, don't just watch yourself go out of business. Second, do some research? Find out what people are serving, how much they are charging, and how long does it take to get in and out for lunch. Time is very important for lunch, as no one wants to be late back to work because you don't have a clue. Third, loose the soup or salad option, one pickle spear, the other two are just a waste of money, reduce the amount of fries to what one human being can consume, loose the dessert course, keep the price, as it is competitive, and get your prep time down to 10-12 minutes. This as usual, is just my opinion.

This restaurant, I found out is owned by a chain that is not local and wants to be in this market. These guys better get it together soon and it will become a very short chain here in Florida.

Welcome to the new millennium. Software solutions are the key to a successful operation. Often times as a server, we are challenged to accommodate customers with special orders. This is not supposed to be difficult or present problems for the servers or the kitchen. There is no such thing as SEE SERVER! As a server, programmer, data base genius with CSS and HTML knowledge, and a whole lot of POS Systems experience, I am probably a little more competent to talk about this subject at length than most. Regardless which POS system you are using, it can always be improved. Who wants to type "egg whites" on the keyboard every time someone orders them or type in "no wrap" for a wrapped item, when there should be a modifier button? This makes the old manual system look more appealing. But even hand writing dupes and tickets needs some level of organization. Abbreviations are key when taking orders and submitting dupes. The same or better level of organization should be present for sophisticated POS Systems.

First, the system should flow so the same path that you take your order is the same way you ring it in. 1, 2, 3, and 4. I.e. eggs, meat, starch, toast. If it doesn't, then it takes you more time at each junction of the serving process.

Second, make a "wouldn't it be easier if" list and have everyone in your establishment help critique, complete and tweak it. For example have a Baked Potato key for entrees, and Egg Whites key for an omelet and a selection of Cheese modifiers for the burgers.

Third, find someone or some way to get this done. For most Mom and Pop operations, this will be a challenge. For larger organizations, there is usually someone talented in this area. If you are really lucky, your restaurant will have a contract with the POS provider that can do all this work for you. It is important to exactly communicate to the programmer what you want. Remember most or some programmers have never waited tables before and they only know programming. I know one who is great, Kathy. She has served and managed restaurants for many years and she almost knows what I want, when I start speaking. I am a lucky man.

Forth, get it done.

Talk to your peers, Chefs, and other important people, like your boss and be sure everyone is in agreement. Go back and tweak the list and identify who will perform this task. Remember that, if this is completed correctly there are fewer mistakes, extra items are properly charged for, sales will increase, turnover will improve and guess what, and you will make more money. I almost always ring higher sales and wait on more people than my peers every day. I also make more money than they do. Uh! It's all about the turnover, Turn and Burn Baby! It's the secret to success. Of course I have an advantage where I work because I do most of the programming whenever we need to make changes and I always have Kathy if I get stuck. See, we have a contract.

Make it verses buy it and save money! Want to make a pile of cash, and then read on. For novices and experts this post will save you money. I hope it gets you to at least, think. Everytime someone touches your food before it reaches your loading dock, it cost you money. How much can you save, how about 10% of your profit? Get your calculator handy as I will take you through some cost savings that will make you go Hmmm!

Let's say I am the prep cook you don't have. I make $15 per hour. You buy boneless skinless chicken breast, already pounded and ready to use for $4 a pound. Let's say you use 100# per week. Now you can buy random chicken breast for about $2 a pound and in one hour I can give you the same or a better product in about an hour. So in one hour you paid me $15 to save you $200. Are you with me? You buy salad dressings already made. I can make them from scratch, giving you a better product and save you $6 a gallon. You use 6 different types. It takes me an hour and you pay me $15 and I save you $21. Cut fruit is a good example. I know you think your staff and high paid chefs don't have the time for this but, $2 a pound vs. $1 a pound and I use about 100# a week. I just saved you $85 as you paid me $15 to save you $100. Bag your own wings, make your own crab cakes, I could go on and on, but I think you get the point. So I am your prep cook and I save you $50 for every hour I work. I work 2000 hours a year. That's $100,000 a year in savings. Less $30,000, my salary, I save you $70,000 a year, right? Do you hire me? Some Chefs may want to do the work themselves, as you know how Chefs can be. If they tell you they don't have time because of business volume, then the prep cook is the answer, or maybe even a dishwasher with some spare time and some skills with a knife.

Look at your food cost and I certainly hope you take inventory and have a food cost number. The biggest feature about knowing your food cost is to the evaluate waste and, yes, theft. Improving your food cost can get you to the Bahamas for four weeks, paid. Ignoring it will keep you in your restaurant day and night, 7 days a week for the rest of your life. I also run a consulting firm that gives the first consultation FREE. You need to have an accounting system, I recommend QuickBooks, and remember, this business is not a hobby, and it's a profession!

17

How to Make Money

It's a busy morning on a Sunday on the holiday weekend. The restaurant is full except for one deuce. A regular couple arrives and takes the table. I see them arrive and watch the busser get them two glasses of water. I observe this out of the corner of my eye and figure less than one minute has passed. I always have a running stop watch going in my head. The busser tells me they are ready to order. Really! The busser reminds me again that they are ready to order. High expectations? I don't think you can get to the microphone of a drive through restaurant in less than a minute. Time appears to fly when you have nothing to do. This couple never talks to each other as many don't every day. To be blind to the fact that there are 100 other people, who are in the restaurant, is either ignorant or inconsiderate. I drop what I am doing and take care of them and they are in and out. That is just what they wanted. People who come in and are busy talking or having a meeting don't seem to notice or care how much time passes, as we are always fast and efficient.

Recognize couples who don't speak and try to move them up in the order of your stuff to do list.

Perform this exercise the next time you get a group of people together for a meeting or a seminar. Have your group do absolutely nothing for ninety seconds. Make sure there are no clocks in the room. I mean nothing, no cell phones, no talking, just nothing. At the end of the 90 seconds, ask each individual how much time has passed. I think you will be surprised at the different answers. This shows how people perceive time when they are not doing anything which is how a customer feels when they are waiting in a restaurant to have their order taken.

I've been in a great mood lately as things in my life are finally start to turn around in a very positive way. This week I decided to project my good mood in my job with my customers. After greeting my tables with the usual stuff, I always ask how everybody is. Most of the time they respond with a mediocre answer and most of the time they ask me how I am. All week I have been responding with the word "Perfect"! I have been getting some interesting looks from this answer all week. There have been raised eye-brows, dropped jaws and a look that almost ask, "Why is he so good today and how can he be perfect? They usually just let it go. Have you ever tried to make someone you know smile when you know they are in a bad mood and it works? They finally crack a smile and you have done a good thing. I don't know if I had an impact on my customers this week or not, but I think I at least left them pondering.

Try this tomorrow or in the next few days. Blow people away when they ask you how you are. Use words like fabulous, excellent, outstanding or perfect. I guarantee you will get some kind of response even if it's not verbal. Make somebody smile tomorrow! By the way tips are up this week. Do you think there is any connection? If this works for you, do it every day for the rest of your life. Your life will improve I guarantee it.

After reading an article in the Wall Street Journal, on February 22, 2012 entitled "How Waiters Read a Table to Adapt Service", it prompted me to write this. I only want to talk about two things today. One is the greeting and the other is getting people's attention.

The greeting of "hello my name is ####, and I will be your server today, I agree is out dated. I prefer to greet, take a drink order and let them know who I am and if they need anything today, do not hesitate to ask me. It just flows for me better. We have also been instructed to use the "Welcome to Firehouse" greeting to all guests, everytime. My problem with this is 75% of our guests are repeat customers. I prefer, good morning Marty or Harold or Max, how are you today? After all, they do come in 7 days a week. At the Half Shell Oyster House, servers are instructed to write their name on the paper lining on each and every table. Very effective as now management knows someone has been to the table and the guests won't forget your name. David, a waiter at the Half Shell, practiced writing his name upside down so the guests can read it. Try it it's not that hard.

Getting people's attention I agree is more of an art than a science. I prefer the eye contact method. When I make the initial contact, I hold that eye contact, smile and go directly to the table. You can't always make eye contact with people in a meeting or lovers staring in each other's eyes. If I get there, I wait for a break in the conversation to start my service. I agree being ignored seems like an eternity, so sometimes you just have to break into a conversation. If you do this correctly, you can take control of the dining experience. After all they did come in to eat. I do however disagree with putting your palms on the table technique. I don't approve of crouching down to take orders either. Most of the time I think crouching and palms on the table is unprofessional. Proper salutation with the right amount of diction, volume, and eye contact should let your guests know that you are in charge of this time segment of the day and everytime you return, you are in control.

Never ask a "Yes or No" question.

This is a seminar I conducted years ago to help servers and bartenders increase check average, hence income.

Bartenders, heads up.

A drink is ordered. Your response is to list all the premium options as opposed to settling for the house brand. I.e. Scotch on the rocks. Would you like Chivas, Dewar's, Glenlevit or J & B.? It's not a yes or no question and sometimes peer pressure in a bar will upsell the customer to keep his peers from thinking he is not frugal. Don't ask "Do you want" ask "Which would you prefer".

Food servers, heads up.

Try to go the entire process without asking a Yes or No question. For appetizers tonight I suggest Shrimp Cocktail, Baked French Onion Soup, or Crab cakes, what would you like to start with tonight? If that doesn't work, suggest something to split or for the table. For entrées, suggest the most expensive item, cheese or bacon on the burger, add side dishes like asparagus or anything that is extra. For wine, make suggestions, I recommend a bottle of Shiraz or Malbec with your meal, which one can I get for you. Not asking yes or no questions prompts the customer to select or to construct a sentence which tells you they do not want to upgrade. When the meal is served don't ask if everything is okay, Ask "How is everything?" It makes them choose a word from their vocabulary to describe how everything is. Repeat the process with dessert offering mouthwatering descriptions of your favorites, or your entire dessert menu. Follow that with "who would like to start". Coffees, cappuccinos and after dinner drinks follow, use the same procedure. After you have cranked the bill up as far as you can, I have not figured out how not to ask if they are ready for the check which IS a "Yes or No" Question. I just put it on the table.

Results

Higher check averages results in higher tips. The establishment also benefits by higher revenues. It's a win win situation. Try It. Good Luck!

This is the question "How far are we willing to go to please the guest?" The real question is when we say "NO". There is a rule in this business regarding exceptions. You have to have the ingredients, it must be reasonable for the kitchen to prepare it, and it must be cost effective. That means not too much labor or too much cost to the quest. Remember the word REASONABLE! Let me give you some examples. A guest wants

Chicken Parmesan. It's not on the menu; however we have chicken, red sauce, cheese and pasta. The problem is, on a busy day, no one has time to thaw out a chicken breast, set up a breading station, sauté the chicken, heat the red sauce, pasta, etc, etc. This is not reasonable. So we say NO. Another example is a Grilled Ham and Cheese Sandwich. We have all the ingredients and it is no skin off anyone back to prepare this item, we say YES. Last Sunday I saw an order of chips and Salsa on a table, not on the menu. The server used Bagel Chips (we use for soup) and the Salsa for the breakfast burrito. Not too bad but how much do we charge, $1, $4, $6. Does anyone know what this item cost and what we should charge for it? Lastly, friends of a server came in asked if she could strain the pulp out of the orange juice. Really! That's a big NO! On a Sunday morning in the middle of serving 500 people for breakfast, who has time to do that? This requires a China Cap and two different containers from the back kitchen. Total prep time is 6 minutes. No one has spare time like that on a Sunday. Not reasonable. When you are busy, tell your friends NO. If they truly are your friends, they will understand.

Learn your kitchen inside and out. Know what all the ingredients are available to you, not an easy task. If you are not sure how to make the call, Yes or No, ask someone who has been there a while, especially the chef. He is the one that is going to make your exception. Time is always important as when it is slow, we probably do more for people than when it is busy. The side effect of this is that sometimes when people get exceptions once, (when it's slow), they expect it anytime, like when it's busy. You'll hear "I get it here all the time here". This is where the yeses screw up the nos.

Every table you greet, you have to read the table and figure how to address the guest. There are several choices and you need to decide to use something that you are comfortable with as well as the guests. Gender is important, so for men you can use gentleman, boys, sirs or guys. For women you can use ladies, girls, Maam and not guys. They are not guys. However according to Wikipedia; *"you guys* - in the U.S.,particularly in Midwest, Northeast, West Coast, Canada, and in Australia; regardless of the genders of those referred to" is acceptable. I personally don't like the term and I know some older people and women take offense to the term "guys". Folks are very southern and y'all just doesn't seem appropriate in a restaurant. Everyone, this term works well if you have a large group of three or more.

Choose your words carefully. I have been criticized by older women for calling them girls and others just love it. Find something you are comfortable with and go with it. It's your first impression, so don't screw it up. Remember we work for tips.

Figure out what you are dealing with right up front. Make eye contact upon your initial approach. One of six things will happen next. One, if "**Eye Contact**" is returned, then you are in good shape. If you get the second, **"The Look Away"**, you are probably dealing with someone who is not is sales and probably has a recessive personality. Third is **The Friendly** response. This is your best shot at having a good dining experience both on your end and theirs. Forth is the "**Business Look**", all business and is interested in closing the deal and the meal is secondary. Fifth is the "**What are you doing here look**". It is okay, just go in the kitchen and say, what the ***## do you think I'm doing here, you moron. The sixth is "**The No Nonsense Look**". This is just your basic "Get er done" customer that wants to eat and run. The point here is to know what you are dealing with and how to act accordingly. You obviously are not going to laugh it up with "**No Nonsense** or the **Business** guest.

Make that eye contact and see what happens. Practice reading this so you don't waste your time trying to be friendly and spending too much time at a table that doesn't require it.

Flirting is probably one of the oldest practices ever. It's done everywhere including the hospitality business. It happens in adult entertainment clubs, bars, restaurants and everywhere else in this industry as well as in life in general. It is defined as a temporary playful romance, or a brief involvement or casual interest, a short playful action based on a lighthearted feeling, or participating in something in a superficial way. Sometimes it suggests a sexual interest, even in the smallest way. We do it in this business to increase tips. Removing the "it's never going to happen" aspect when interacting with guests, leads members of the opposite sex, to imagine, assume, fanaticize, or create false hopes about the flirter. People return time and time again to see their favorite server in hopes that the next step will occur. It most cases it will probably not. You keep leading them on because money is the key to happiness. It even happens to old guys like me.

Two women came in to dine today and I am started with "you look familiar". How old is that line. Two women in their 50"s, attractive are having lunch together. I am bored and alone so I decide to play this out. I have a quick tongue and can think on my feet. At first it was fun and then it was more fun. I don't know what signal I was sending but the result was a 40% tip. I doubt they will be back for me, but if they do I will play along again.

Go for it every day. Keep up the compliments, i.e., you look sharp, great to see you and the like. Your income depends on it. As long as it doesn't get creepy, you should be okay.

Ever have one of those weekends where absolutely nothing goes wrong? I just did. Busy, busy, busy is the only way to describe it. One employee short on Saturday, and just balls to the wall slamming, non-stop, busy. Sunday, my day off, someone calls in sick and I figure that the temperature has dropped 20 degrees in one day and the wind is constant at 27 MPH, that there would be no outside business (40 seats), but I go in any way. Well once the inside dining area filled up everyone else sat outside. Another tidal wave is upon us and it just doesn't stop. Folks just keep coming and coming. Everyone is doing their best and there really are no problems. I love it when a plan comes together. Everything is spot on and there are NO MISTAKES, so to speak. It's a great feeling. When everyone is "in the zone" it's like you're in an" Iron Eagle and nothing can hurt you". The day results in big sales and big bucks for the servers. Great job everyone!

Days like this have huge residual effects. You are pumped for a few days afterwards, smile all the way to the bank, and morale is way up. We all have had bad days, especially me lately with no time off lately, but it is great to have a pair of back to back perfect days. I love my job!

The key to this business is how to be effective all the time. I can't help to make reference to the team, any sport, basketball, football or your restaurant team. In all my years of management, it is knowing when to be in the operation and when to be in the office. As a server it's knowing when to take a cigarette break and when to help your team succeed. Non-team players, whether vocalized or not, we know who you are. The definition of management is "controlling events". You can make or break any situation. 30 minutes helping out during a lunch rush goes a lot farther than being somewhere less important. It's the success of your operation that depends on it. Recalling a story from years ago as a manager would have lunch after the lunch rush, usually 2:00 0'clock. As business declined, the manager keep eating lunch earlier and earlier until the manager was having lunch at noon. Instead of addressing the problem as why lunch was so slow, the manager continued to ignore the symptom. Eventually he got fired. Remember without guests, we have no business.

WOW! What a Tsunami today! Its noon and not much is going on and then, Boom!!! It's busy; but its lunch hour so no big deal. Things are going well and then it happened. I screwed up. Two tables decide to pay at the same time. One is a party of seven and the other is a deuce. They are all separate checks. It's mostly credit card and a couple of cash payments. Somehow I switched the credit cards at the two tables. Major mistake! Now, in the middle of this Tsunami, I have to fix four credit card mistakes. It's not just two because; I have to retrieve both of my mistakes, delete them and then reprocess them completely. It takes about four minutes but I don't have that kind of time. The first wave is leaving and the second wave is now sitting down. I tell myself I can do this, but in all honesty I wish I would wake up and this nightmare was over. If you have been paying attention for a while you realize how much I can do in four minutes. Okay, I am now officially lost. Thanks to the support of my teammates I survive.

It was an exciting day and I am now consuming a nice Cabernet with my friend Julie and I have the day off tomorrow. Life just gets better every day, not worse. Just start to believe that. Once it's over, let it be and don't take it home with you. You and I will be just fine. Nice Bouquet.

This is definitely one of the busiest and most memorable days of my career of waiting tables. It's Sunday, busiest day of the week and 4 servers are scheduled and we are always busy after church lets out 11:00am-1:00pm. There are two openers

@7:00am, one at 8:00am and one at 9:00am. At 7:10 I realize my opening partner is late and I shift into high gear. At 8:00 I see a note from the closing bartender that she will be in at 8:30. At 8:15 I get a call from the 9:00 explaining how sick she is and won't be in. Wow, doesn't this look like it's going to be a fun day!! 110 seats total, inside and the patio for only two servers, apparently the other opener is not coming in (her last day). What to do?

Change into your sneakers, put on your game face, and bring on you're A Game. We each have 10 tables each inside and 5 tables outside on the humid patio, where people bring their dogs to eat in the Florida summer heat and humidity. As a server, you are expected to perform many tasks all at one time. Organization is the key and extreme organization is needed today. The following is a list of things you need to organize, prioritize, shuffle and reshuffle for the next six hours. The list constantly changes, as every second you need to change the order of the list.

1. Approach table, greet and get drink orders.
2. Run drinks
3. Take food orders including the special requests.
4. Ring food orders.
5. Perform second steps, i.e. get pastries, biscuits, and make toast,

cappuccinos, and lattes, hot teas, etc
6. Run food.
7. Refill beverages
8. Drop checks.
9. Process credit cards.
10. Process discounts and coupons.
11. Return credit card checks for signatures.
12. Make change for cash checks, self cashiering operation.
13. Answer phone, answer stupid questions.
14. Take and process to-go orders, including bagging, check payment and condiments.
15. Be nice!

Remember I'm doing this for 15 tables for six hours, and so is my partner. They wonder why servers drink so much. Every step and every second in this situation is crucial, so perfect planning of every move is essential. Otherwise you're DONE. After a few hours my brain feels like a scrambled egg in a stainless steel bowl with the Chef whipping it with a wire whisk as fast as he can. Surge on as closing time is inevitable. The owner strolls in somewhere in the middle of this, grabs an apron and pretends to wait tables. This is pretty much like spitting in the ocean and expecting the tide to change. It looked like he was trying to help.

Day is done and we survived. The place is a wreck and it looks like they may be giving last call at the local watering hole before we get done cleaning up. We close at 2:00pm. That's right 2:00pm. Sales were great and my partner and I rang twice what we would have on a normal day. We tip out the Busser and the Expo, great help, (no sarcasm for a change) and leave with a good chunk of change. Was it worth it? I'll let you decide. The last time I had to do that is July 4 last year when alcohol related incidents caused two servers to be 2 ½ hours late each. That day was just as memorable. It took us three hours to clean up and reset for the next day. We still made the bar in plenty of time before closing.

Always expect the unexpected. I do prep work a day out because in the event something like this happens and you have to pull a lonely shift again, you are better prepared. Think, Grasshopper, **what to do when**, look at the list again, which requires constant concentration and thinking. Remember most customers don't give us the credit we're due.

Name recognition is great ways to increase your tips, making people feel special like the TV show "Cheers. People want to go "Where Everybody Knows You Name".

Regulars;

People come in almost every day and if you don't know their name. Ask them. You're a server. It's what you do!! Learn their names and what the like, i.e. coffee flavor, spicy, the daily special or the same mundane thing every day. Phil, decafe, egg white omelet, spinach, mushrooms, and cheddar with berries and Sourdough toast. And don't forget the glass of water and expect a MasterCard. That's how you make primo bucks. Remember as you follow this blog you will learn lots of little things, but added together, you can double your income on a yearly basis. Yes I said DOUBLE!

Credit cards;

Credit card payments provide you with names, lots of names! Use them. Name use is a little tricky as it depends on what kind of atmosphere you work in, casual or formal. In a business hotel I would use last names unless the name has more consonants than vowels in it. In a casual atmosphere if YOU think first names are appropriate than, do it. It will surprise them and impress them and you know, more tips. By the way TIPS means several things, but my favorite is "to insure prompt service". If you get a bad tip, think why. Maybe you did something wrong. It helps us learn. Hey, I've made mistakes and have suffered the consequences, but I have learned from it. I have learned to circle things on my order pad that I forget or have missed in the past so it doesn't happen again.

A woman I work with tried this one day, learning everyone's name, as the day wore on, and she matched me in tips even though she rang 20% less than I did. Maybe it works.

Make notes, listen and learn Grasshopper, I've been doing this for 200 years and some of this stuff actually works. If you don't try it, you will never know.

Let's make a pile of cash. Every day I wake up with the intent to have a super day, money wise. Sometimes people just get in my way. There is mister Wi-Fi. He has no office and intends to spend all day taking up one of your tables, I mean all day, as in 6 hours. This is the guy who orders food to make his presence justified. Is it really fair to me for one person to take up a four top for two meal periods for a $10 check? He sponges power from the wall at his table as by now the battery in his laptop is in need of a charge. He spends most of his stay on his cell phone and it is difficult to talk with him as I get the feeling that I am intruding or interrupting. I really don't care if you're talking to your boss. Are suppose to be in your office, than go. This guy is a regular and is not helping send my kid through college. I now ask him to move to the counter or a smaller table as I cannot afford to have him hanging out all day, especially during the lunch rush.

We are not a Match.com meeting place. If this is your first date and things are going so well, get a room or take it to the next step. Don't spend two hours in my section getting to know each other. I don't charge rent, I make tips. Two cups of coffee and a muffin is not my idea of a meal. If I take you to breakfast or lunch, I will buy you your own meal. When I am busy, my policy is "Here is your check, now go".

The key to high sales and tips is turnover. Turn and burn. I don't want a bunch of Match.com and Wi-Fi people in my station all fricking day. I make more money than most of my coworkers because I am fast with everything, order taking, food service and check presentation. So eat and boogie. The only advice I can offer is keep bussing the table and keep offering drink refills and hope that they get the hint. Mo money my friends.

18

Occupations

The Hostess

This position controls your life as a server. His or her position's objective is to get everyone in and out and to have no one left to seat, every day. This position also takes some crap from guests. Things like I had a reservation did not, and I am not waiting past my expected time. Well stuff happens. Meetings run over and the man proposing marriage to his girlfriend usually runs over the expected average dining time. So somehow you have to figure a nice way to tell the guests that are waiting for tables to be still and shut up. An experienced host (hostess) controls the blood flow of the restaurant. They need to insure proper station rotation, so as not to weed any one server, while trying to maximize seating capacity. So the goal, which is a difficult one to achieve, is to make everyone happy. How easy is that?

Lighten up a little on your hostess. They deal with reservations, impatient people, food complaints and you and me. Have a heart.

The Expeditor

This position is the key to keep you from going under when the shit hits the fan. If you figure 300-400 people will come through your doors in seven hours on a Saturday or a Sunday, there needs to be a stress buffer for everyone to survive. That is this position. He buffers all the bullshit that is created by servers, chefs, dishwashers, busser and anyone else who adds to the situation. You don't need 6 people talking to the chefs, talk to the expeditor. You don't need the chefs hunting down 5 servers either, talk to the expeditor. The expeditor is the marriage counselor of the entire crew. It's a tough job keeping all those tickets in order, dealing with all the SPERCIAL ORDERS, keeping all the toast on the right plate and selling tables as fast as you can. I used to do that job and not enough credit is given to the individual in this position.

Just once I would like to switch this job with ANY server for a day, to appreciate how difficult this job really is. Love your EXPO or you could be doing it next week if you don't!

The Busser

This position is designed to clear and reset tables. It never seems to work out that way. Even when I was a busser four decades ago, it hasn't changed. This is this person that catches all the shit that no one has time to do or wants to do. You are asked to go above and beyond the call of duty and usually no one appreciates you. They just take you for granted. It seems like everytime the busser stops for a minute to take a break; someone comes along with something to do. It could be a manager, a chef or anyone. You'll do it too cause you ARE the busser. This is the person who gets your side of mayonnaise when you forget or cleans up your spill when you don't have time. They get your drinks when you don't have time and usually helps in ways that definitely is not their job. The only way out of this quandary is getting promoted to a server. Then you have a new busser to use and abuse.

Love your busser as they are priceless especially when you are slammed. Tip them well and a few extra bucks will always make them feel a little more appreciated.

The Dishwasher

Here is another unappreciated job. It's where I started over forty years ago. It is your job to wash just about everything that gets used. You are also expected to do anything that anyone asked you, like the busser, but in the back of the house. You mop up spills that are not yours and you are constantly expected to help everyone when they need help. You do prep work for the chef, make pastries in your spare time, take the trash out to the dumpster which is 300 feet away and yes, fetch food for everybody from the storeroom which is 400 feet away. This person usually never takes a break, eats standing up in the dish room and only goes to the bathroom when it is absolutely necessary. It's a non-stop position but it's a job. It's the only one I could get back then and it's even harder to find jobs today.

The only positive upside to this position is it could be a launching pad for upward mobility. I went from dishwasher, to bus, to cook, to server all in the same restaurant. So there is hope. Hey guys, be nice to your dishwasher. Think about this, if he walks out, you're *@#/ed.

The Bartender

Out with friends last night, I fell in love again with the bartender, the job, not the person. It was a busy downtown location and a Saturday night so it was busy. Four bartenders were working like orangutans. I used to be a bartender in busy clubs when in college and a few other places. The hardest bartending job I had was working at a Tiki Bar/ Lobby Bar. It was two bars. One was in the lobby and when you turned around and took two steps you were out at the pool. During Spring Break, which in Florida is a state holiday, it last 3 weeks. It's all about Pina Coladas, Rum Runners, Mojitos and all kinds of frozen drinks not to mention the food, Burgers, Chicken Fingers and Chicken Wings. This job requires a great deal. It requires, extreme coordination, as you have to multi-task constantly to survive. You need to be the best on the cash register; you need to know a million drink recipes and you have to keep your smile all day. The result is a whole lot of money. Last night reminded me of this as the fantastic 4 were, as bartenders call it "Doing the Dance". For hours they were weaving in and out of each other's way in a bar that stretched almost 100 feet long but hardly 3 feet wide. They were mixing drinks, shots, changing kegs, taking cash and running tabs. And they were all smiling and we all know why, money.

Next time you are out in a busy bar, watch that special individual and watch them "Do the Dance". I was tipping 30% all night and I am sure the people I was with were doing the same, as we were all hospitality peeps. A good bartender can easily make over $1000 a week. They are worth every penny, because not everyone has the skill set to perform this job. Be sure to take care of your bartenders.

Chefs

Chefs are unique people. This individual has always been a person of special needs.

They need constant stroking, are seldom wrong, and are usually right, always perfect and extremely moody. They all need to have more sex! Most of them like to stick to their curriculum, hate exceptions, don't really give two shits about what the customer wants and really don't care about your tips. Usually when they screw up, you suffer when it comes time to leaving a tip. A lady last week paid her check and shorted me on the bill. She claimed that last week she had to send her steak back because it wasn't cooked to her desired doneness. That was last week and I had nothing to do with her steak. I didn't ask about the lack of a tip, but she offered to tell me I wasn't getting one because of last week's food experience.

Chefs usually complain about everything. They hate it when you sell a bunch of stuff and you run out. Now they have to make more. Well next time, make it suck and I won't sell it because over time people won't order it because it sucks. They complain there is always too much work and not enough time. They also think they are God's gift to the opposite sex and can usually walk on water. BMC stands for Bitch, Moan and Complain. I am lucky, as my breakfast Chef is great and only has a few of the previously mentioned faults. My night Chefs on the other hand have all the qualities mentioned above. Luckily I don't work too many nights.

Kiss some ass. Your income depends on it. You won't win an Ego battle with a Chef. You will just get grief. I have found that he or she is the best person to make your friend. By the way, my advice is to never date a chef. That would just cause a host of problems for you, the rest of the entire staff, the chef, and the entire restaurant operation. Trust me on this one.

Managers

Not a lot of people like their boss and that is understandable. They control a lot of your life. They schedule unfairly, make demands that seem unreasonable, ride you needlessly, schedule you to work shifts you don't want to work, like holidays, etc. etc. There are some good bosses out there, but it really wouldn't be any fun talking about them now would it. I have described the different types on manages in a previous chapter.

Partners

Just when you think it can't any worse, it does. Right now everything is perfect. You are busy but you are not missing a beat. A silent, or should be silent partner, walks in the middle of a few people doing a great job and starts asking stupid questions about irrelevant stuff not realizing what is going on. This person has 40 years of experience and still doesn't have a clue. Someone is always charging their cell phone and someone's pocketbook is always in the wrong place. The coffee grinder needs a half of bag of decaf beans; it holds three bags and the cello-wrapped toothpicks need to be fuller than it is. Something needs to be cleaned, but not right now, but sometime in the near future. This is not the place or time for all this shit. Scotty please beam her out, NOW. Why do people always try to knock you off your perch? I think that it makes them feel superior when they make you feel inferior. These are just my thoughts. Finally the silent partner grabs some free food and a fresh drink and becomes silent, after the damage has been done.

The chef is still harping on the wrong pancake order from 3 hours ago and lunch is slammed to boot. The only good news is that this day is almost over as I can't wait for the night crew to get there. Most of the people who work here can't handle the stress. Support and positive reinforcement is seldom present in my atmosphere. That's why someone invented alcohol. It's for servers to drink after work. Shake it off unless you can find a better job. Rest well my friends as tomorrow the silent partner may not show up.

Servers

I have worked with servers of all ages over the years and found some common differences based on age. I will expand my observations between a 19 year old and a 39 year old server. The first is punctuality. At nineteen, you sleep as little as possible only to make to work just in time, not to be late. At thirty-nine you get as much sleep as possible and always show up early as to never be late. The second is drinking. At nineteen, you drink as much as possible every night, as late as possible, only to make sure that you are barely functional at work the next day. At thirty-nine, you drink only to your limit or as little as possible to make sure you are fully functional at work the next day. The next is dating. At nineteen, you ask questions of your fellow workers like, do you think he is single, I don't see a ring? You give your phone number to everyone that you think is a prospect. At thirty-nine, you give your phone number to no-one, as you know there is no relationship to be found with anyone you wait on in the restaurant and that all members of the opposite sex are creeps. The last is flirting. At nineteen you flirt to get a date. At thirty-nine you flirt to make money.

The thirty-nine year shows up with their A game, with a positive attitude, and the desire to make lots of money. The nineteen year old shows up with their B or C game, hoping they can just make it through the day. Think about this the next time you are out. The bartender that is thirty-nine, who is flirting with you, is only doing it to make money. The nineteen year old server, who is flirting with you, is wondering if you would be a good catch. Think about it. At my age, I am always on time, never drink too much, and only flirt to make money.

Who do you like working with? I like working in an environment where they are always there for you, day or night, greet you everytime like they haven't seen you in weeks. They are always by your side and there when you need them. They always perform any task asked of them. They are never out sick or are never late. They trust you implicitly and never talk back. They never bitch, complain or fail to please. Dedication is a hard quality to find these days and some who are dedicated show it every minute of every day. You can confide in them and they will never repeat what you have told them. They always have a look of interest on their faces when you speak. This is whom I want to be surrounded by every day.

I have found these qualities and cherish them every day. I thank God for bringing them into my life. Maybe someday you should meet my DOGS.

19

Miscellaneous

A while ago on a busy Sunday I found a $50 bill on the floor in my station. It was folded in quarters and under a table. As I always look at the condition of my station I noticed it and picked it up. It was a brand new party at the table so it is unlikely that they dropped it. If the party that just left dropped it, they are long gone. What I am I to do? I figured I would hold on to it for the rest of the day, to see if anyone returned to claim it. One Sunday I dropped a $20 bill out of my pocket while making change. A customer picked it up and returned it. They saw it, they knew where it came from, they were honest, and they gave it back to me. Thank you.

When I lived in New York City, I found a money clip on Broadway and 44th street. I picked it up. It had $847 in it. I kept it. What was I to do? Sorry, I spent it. No one ever returned to claim the fifty dollar bill either so I spent that too.

Water is an important part of life. It is the largest ingredients in most everything in the world that we consume. It is in beer, wine, liquor and most foods. By itself it can be fascinating. People drink it from bottles, fountains, filters on their faucets, filter bottles and some right from the tap. People have it delivered to their homes and offices, refill it at vending machines and some just chug it from a gallon jug. It can be sparkling, from a foreign country or still, from a mountain somewhere in this country. It is ordered, more frequently than you think, in restaurants with or without ice, with or without lemon, extra lemon(if you are too frugal to pay for lemonade), and some people order it HOT, because they either brought their own tea bag or are concocting their own beverage. One customer brought in his own powdered Starbuck Mix and added it to my hot water. He used my cream and sugars, my cup and spoon, which someone has to wash at the end of the day and I can't charge him for anything. This just doesn't seem fair. It's like the woman who ordered iced water in a to-go cup. So now there is the cup, lid, straw, lemon, and ice, all for a charge of Nada. Hey 8 cents of nothing adds up over time if you do the math.

In the state where I live, you have to request water; it cannot just be brought to you. It's a conservation thing. I am certain that as time goes on and the planet, on which we live, gets more screwed up, there will be a charge for water to cover those escalating cost of disposable wares and condiments. Remember, everything relates back to the price of oil. Petroleum products are used in the production of the previously mentioned items and if not, it still cost to fuel the trucks that have to deliver them. Someone told me once you can write an article about water!

This is an update to the recent road construction happening in front of my restaurant. Business really hasn't changed as we are out of season in Florida now and things are slowing down. I have no complaints. The current issue is with commuters. What used to be an easy way to get to work is no longer that way. People have struggled to find an alternative way to work and some have figured out a shortcut. The shortcut consists of entering one parking lot, traveling behind an office building and through our other parking lot. It's actually is a good solution however someone always has to screw it up. Zipping behind an office building at forty miles per hour is dangerous. If you guys went 15-20 MPH, everything would be cool. The office building is occupied by our landlord. He got peeved and decided to block the latest cool discovery by parking vehicles there.

The logistics is complicated and I won't get into it. The reason I am writing this is because I took a bunch of asschewings today for my landlord's actions. I am sorry for your inconvenience but the city closed the road and the landlord put up the roadblock. I had nothing to do with this.

Get on MapQuest and figure out a new way to get around this problem. I am not happy about this either, as I watch heavy equipment move all day and I feel as though I will make it through this dilemma. I know it is a pain, but figure out two things, how to get to work and the phone number for the city that started this project. I really don't know what to say to you when you complain to me. Chillax my good friend!

Ever had one of those days where everything you do is a struggle. Today is that day. Nothing is going right and everything I do I think is wrong. Things are so bad I have to right down the drink orders. That's bad because it's iced water. One is no ice with lemon, another no ice and no lemon, another with ice and no lemon and another with ice and lemon. One table ordered a Decaf and iced water and when I returned, the other party wanted a Decaf and I would like water now.

Today I don't understand two things. One, is how do you not know what you want to drink? This is not a restaurant where your breakfast or your lunch dictates weather you order a Pinot Grigio or a Pinot Noir. If you drink Iced Tea, than order one, and if you drink Coke, order one. Two, what is with all the iced water today. Are you cheap or do you still believe that drinking 8 glasses of water a day will make you live to be 100 years old? I had one guy today who tried to get the rest of his party to special order. Shut up and wait your turn. Anyway it was a totally challenging day. What you don't know is despite all my problems today, nobody knew. Tips were outstanding and on the outside everything was great. On the inside, it sucked. I couldn't wait for this day to be over.

Live each day as it is your last. I struggled all day but everyone loved me. The day ended on a good note, as all you servers know, "Money Covers all Sins". It's also a pretty good motivator as this will motivate me, probably for the rest of the week.

I am the only male server in the entire collection of waitstaff. It's true everyone is better looking and younger, as I am the oldest of the group, 56 years young. I get a little tired of where is this one and that one today, usually from men. We all have our regulars and mine are female. All the guys want a pretty young thing waiting on them instead of a fossil like me. I thought once that if we split the stations up, male and female, I would do great. We also have call parties, people who request a certain server. This can be frustrating if you working a shift you don't normally work or covering for someone on vacation. When you work in a restaurant where "everybody knows your name, it's hard to make any money if no one wants you to wait on them. As usual I just swallow it and move on to tomorrow.

It's a new day and I approach it with the same freshness that I do every day. Yesterday is gone and I can't do anything about it. I'm sure, or not, that when I am not there, people ask for me all the time. Hey it keeps me going and it's a free country, we all have the right to dream.

Every day we hear phrases referencing foods. Ever wonder where they came from, I do. "Don't cry over spilt milk", "You can't have your cake and eat it too" or how about all the ones related to the chicken family, "Don't put all your eggs in one basket", "What came first, the chicken or the egg?" or my favorite, "If you're going to make an omelet, you have to break a few eggs". If you're drinking beer, what does the term "Chug-A-Lug" have to do with the nuts that hold on your tires? I do get some of them, however like "Red as a Lobster", "You have egg on your face" and, "As American as Apple Pie".

In my daily search to see what's going on in town, I was on Craig's list. A noticed a really cool high paying job, the title is not important, that required that you speak fluent English and Spanish. This job is in the USA and I have a real problem with that. I cannot apply for this opportunity because I am not fluent in a foreign language. It is not a job that deals with immigration, it is a hospitality job! So if I am correct, I have to speak Spanish to communicate with the undocumented immigrants (who don't pay taxes and take jobs from American citizens). This, in my opinion is wrong. I sincerely doubt that there is a job in Mexico that requires you to be fluent in English, It's their country.

I just think there are too many people in our industry, not all, that are paid under the table and do not pay taxes to help pay for all our government spending. One undocumented immigrant in each restaurant, times all the restaurants employing them; times $20,000 a year in salary, at a 25% tax rate is billions of dollars. Enough said! Ekkk!!

I received some disturbing feedback about this recent Blog. I pulled the Blog from the site as some individuals have completely missed the message. My Blogs are not intended or directed at anyone or anything. They are for entertainment purposes only. I have been in this business for forty plus years and what you read in my Blog are "the greatest hits" or "the best of" from my life in this industry. Many of the stories I tell, are not even related to the place where I work now, but more so from past places I have worked. If you are offended by my Blogs you have two choices, don't read them, or comment on them, there is a place for that. I will read your comments and post them if they are appropriate.

My goal is to make you feel better about your job, sympathizing with my experiences, make you laugh, say WOW, help you learn, and hopefully, help you cope better with our lives as servers. If you don't have a comment to post on my Blog, then don't Comment outside this Blog. My site reflects my opinions and that's just what they are, my opinions. To my supporters, keep reading, to those I have offended, stop reading.

I want to talk about the adjectives that describe more. When you ask a customer if they want more coffee there should be two responses, yes or no. Here are a few I thought I would share with you. I have heard, a smidge, a touch, a drop, a topper, a warm-up, another swallow, a splash, a dash more, an inch, and of course just a half. These terms all require the desire of the customer to coincide with the server's interpretation of the term. When I am making a cake and I need salt, is it a pinch or a dash of salt, and what is the measurable difference? If I am moving something and it needs to be a hair closer, really, a hair, elephant or human? Does it matter? Do they build skyscrapers that way?

As I am not a scientist, as I learned during Jury Duty last week, these are very black and white people. Most of us are not. So when I say I am leaving soon, will call you later and we will get together in the near future, I have no idea when any of that will be. I have nothing but hope and a whole lot of maybes. It's like when someone leaves a job and they say "let's keep in touch". It never happens. Lastly it reminds me of my younger years when you break up with someone and they say, "We can still be friends". I never knew what that one meant either.

Has the economy affected the way people tip? Last week I was told people aren't stupid, they really do know. So do they intentionally cheat their server out of their due diligence or is it because they are trying to cut back. Does the household budget meeting go something like this; "We spend $10,000 a year eating out and we can save $500 a year if we just leave the servers 15%". When you call a takeout restaurant, you talk to an employee who probably makes $10.00 per hour. They don't expect tips as they don't survive on them. When you call a full service restaurant at noon, busiest time of the day and occupy 15 minutes of valuable time of a server who has a million things to do, discussing the soup of the day, and the rest of the daily specials, while relaying that information to your work colleuges, I wonder if you realize how much time you are actually consuming. I make about $30 an hour. That is about 50 cents a minute. So it just cost me $7.50 to talk to you to get your order. Now I ring your order, get all your extra stuff and package everything, condiments, silverware, etc. You show up and pay the bill and don't tip.

I make $4.65 an hour PLUS TIPS. Thanks. Try calling McDonalds next time and try to order in advance. The same holds true for people with discounts, coupons, Living Social, or whatever deals you have going on. You get 100% of the chef's and the server's attention. You really should tip on the full amount.

Bite your tongue daily as that is just the way some people are. One person comes in everyday and gets oatmeal to-go. He tips $2. Another person gets the same oatmeal and has been coming in for two years and still leaves nothing. I can't figure people out and some days you would just like to speak out, but you can't. Keep taking the good with the bad, because, fortunately there is more good than bad!

A local news station shows up in the restaurant the other day and wanted to speak to a manager. One is rarely available so I try to assist the best I can. The reporter states that's he's doing an article on how the economy is improving and the amount of patrons frequenting the local restaurants is up 10%. The reporter and his camera man came in to interview guests. Arriving at 9:30 am, the supposed peak of the morning, there are four tables in the restaurant out of twenty. This is hardly up 10%. I explained that business levels are flat year to year and I have not seen any significant change. As I explained in last week's blog, I see people ordering and tipping in a more frugal manner. A quote from the same newspaper made a comment about unemployment that was; "The trend remains unambiguously downwards," an economist at High Frequency Economics. "We think the rate of decline ... is slowing ...". I don't see a positive word in that statement. So there was no one to interview and nothing to support an increase in business, so they departed for destinations unknown to me.

I may be the last person to ask for a positive word and I don't and won't get into politics. I personally don't see any improvement in sales, tips or any other part of the economy that affects me. It might have made a good news piece if he showed up on a Saturday or Sunday morning when it is "Balls to the Walls" all day long. Now that's something to write about.

It's a Sunday and we expect to be busy. I don't like taking reservations as people are usually late, don't show, and we have three locations and some get them wrong. A party calls before 8am and booked a reservation for 13 people at 11:30 (peak time of course) and no one takes a phone number. We build the table and they are you guessed it, a no show. I called the other two locations and you will never guess what I heard. They had called both other stores and made the same reservation and did not show up anywhere. The mistake was NO ONE at any of the stores took a number.

I have learned over time that the more information you take during a reservation, the more likely they are to show up. During Holidays I used to take credit card numbers with expiration dates. Trust me, the changes and cancellations were handled with great diligence as no one wanted to get charged hundreds of dollars for a no-show. At least take a phone number.

Road construction is OVER!! It looked pretty great today. There was no heavy equipment, no cones, no signs and it looked like no one had ever been there. However, a water main broke just after 6:30am this morning and in a matter of hours, after only one day, everything was reversed back to last week. There were back-hoes, cones, signs and lots of help. It didn't affect business and it was busy today. It was better than it has been. It's good to see things back to normal.

Only five weeks of suffering and it is apparent to me, that the road construction had hurt us. Well everything is back to normal, so come visit. I will be waiting for you.

A nice couple comes in, has breakfast and the credit card is declined. I always try to be discreet in these matters and ask the gentleman if he has a different card. He did not and the female decides to pay the $20 bill. The first thing that always amazes me is "the look". You know that look if this has happened to you as a server. It's the "I don't have a clue why my card was declined look". I think most people know their financial situation, credit card status, etc and most banks don't make mistakes. The bill is paid and a $3 tip is left. I ask the question, would the tip had been higher is the card was good? After all I had nothing to do with the card status.

I can't help but wonder what conspired next. If it was a first date and the card was declined and the man didn't have $20 dollars on him, I wonder if there will be a second date. If this was a married couple, I would have liked to have heard the conversation on the way home. Hum?

Everyday people ask me what is good, what is popular and what do you like? If you work in a high priced dinner house, the answer is the most expensive item on the menu, as people always tip based on the percentage of the total check. Therefore the Steak Oscar @ $34.95 answers all three of the original questions. If its lunch or folks are on a time limit, i.e., on their way to the airport, then a Chicken Salad Sandwich on whole wheat with lettuce and tomato, served with chips, is a menu item you will see out of the kitchen in only a few minutes. We also make exceptions everyday to please people, but be careful, be sure you know what your kitchen can do. Suggesting the most popular items is safe, and you know what those are. Remember to describe your recommendations precisely as you don't want to disappoint a customer if they order something you recommended and don't like it.

Recommend things that are the best sellers. You should know or your manager has access to a report that will tell you what those items are. You will always be surprised what the numbers will tell you. Good Luck!

Let's talk about drug use in the workplace. I really don't care what you do during your time off as long as it doesn't affect your performance the next day. However what you do while you are at work does affect me. So if you have been out drinking beyond your limit last night and you think smoking a joint or doing a couple of lines of cocaine on your way to work will help you, I am torque. You arrive at work and give me some lame ass excuse that you have allergies and your eyes look like a Google map and I know your presence in not going to help the operation today. I also know people who drink at work. The smart ones do from their vehicles and the stupid ones do it in the building. There are no breakfast sauces made with wine! So I have a Chef who is coked out, a server who shows up over the legal limit and has smoked a doubie, and a cook who stays drunk all day. Now everyone is not 100% and moody. I am straight and have been down this road before so I know what is going on. Days like this are not the best for me as I just want to make some serious money and go home.

Most restaurants do no employ a "Drug Free" workplace. It's harder to find help if you take out the drugies. So the rest of us will pick up the slack and deal with your inability to perform. It will be a long day as we will deal with the incoherencies and the short tempered barking from the kitchen, but we will again survive.

It's like drinking, do it on your time off and don't bring it to work.

20

My Experiences Out

I don't go out much, as it makes the brain scan too much information, which does not result in a relaxing evening out. I am headed to my local restaurant to enjoy the whole Maine Lobster Special and watch some NCAA basketball. Upon arrival there is a 45 minute to 1 hour wait except at the bar. I'm there. This lobster special used to be $10.98, then $12.98 and now $14.98, all in an eight week period of time. Judging by the wait times, it is still a great deal. You can't make that at home for the same price. It's a good price value as it comes with baked potatoes and coleslaw. I order a beer and some wings as an appetizer, as I know the kitchen is slammed with the dining room and lobster orders.

The bartender is fast, efficient, pleasant and knowledgeable. She is making all kids of FOOFU drinks and a Rusty Nail (a drink from the 50's made with Scotch and Drambuie). She is not very friendly as she is too busy. She is just a well oiled machine, doing what it takes to get the job done. The difference between here and where I work, here it's in and out, never see you again. Where I work it's more of a Cheers atmosphere with lots of repeat guests. My dinner arrives and I am in need of some black pepper. I steal the bartenders name off of my guest check and call her but she does not respond immediately. I call her again and she explained that she is sorry but most customers call her Miss, Excuse Me, Honey, or some other generic term. She said she was not used to people using her name. Dinner is done, check is paid, 30% tip (well deserved) and I depart.

Good dinner and I will return again. It's my regular Wednesday thing and sometimes I go with a date, family, and my son or just alone. It's consistent and you get what you expect. Kudos to the bartender, keep up the good work.

Out for lunch on a day off can be brutal for any establishment I visit. I had lunch at a national chain, no names, and starts with an "A". It seems that the bigger the place, number of units, not seats, the more screwed up things are. Does it really take 12 minutes to get two drinks, it shouldn't. Does it also take 30 minutes to cook Fish and Chips and some Grilled Shrimp, it shouldn't. It shouldn't, but it did. We reordered drinks, big mistake, and another 12 minutes, ate lunch and after we begged for the check and almost 90 minutes had past. We were in no hurry so it really didn't matter. If it took 90 minutes to serve lunch where I work, we wouldn't be in business very long. It's all about speed. Managers look at your ticket times for food and drinks, and then brainstorm how to fix it!

If I am in a hurry or only have an hour for lunch next time, I'm not going to the big "A". We left the server a 100% tip. After all, none of this was her fault. It wasn't busy. I don't get it sometimes.

We were spending a day with another couple at SeaWorld, visiting from New York, a day of fun leads to the need for food. We enter a restaurant on the premises and order cocktails and peruse the menu. The entrée selection is not exciting so we order a series of appetizers. After the waitress realizes that we are not ordering entrees, she turns belligerent. She should have read my blog "Never Judge a Book by Its Cover". Service becomes slow and its takes a flare gun to get her attention to get a second drink. Some people are just in the wrong business. A family of four is seated next to us, ordering kids meals and burgers and I am sure our bill is higher than theirs. I am perturbed by our treatment and my friend and I argue over the bill. I insist, because I want to teach this girl a lesson in the tip. The bill is $74.99 and I whip out my American Express card and boldly round up the bill to $75, leaving her a penny. After all TIPS stands for, **T**o **I**mprove **P**rompt **S**ervice.

To the waitress; Hey get up tomorrow and realize that your day's income depends on your sales, your total sales. Whatever it takes, kids meals, appetizers or whatever, swallow it and have a prosperous day. Lose the attitude and you will make a decent living. I tried to complain to the manager on the way out but after waiting ten minutes, no one showed up so we departed.

I have never heard a server say so little in such a long time frame. The greeting consisted of two letters, Hi. Then there is the look with the order pad out indicating, would you like to order something. My date and I order two iced teas and they are fetched. She returns with the same poised order pad and pen out ready to take the food order. Again nothing is said. We order lunch and within a reasonable amount of time the food arrives. There is no "Enjoy your meal", "can I get you anything", etc., etc. The bill is dropped on the table as most people; I know, don't order dessert at lunch, and again nothing is said. I feel as if I just went through I drive through window.
Unless I looked at the check I wouldn't even know her name.

If you want to spend your life making 10-15% in tips then so be it. If you added a little personality and showed some enthusiasm, you could be doing 20-30%. Think about that next time you feel about being reserved with your guests.

After a very long morning of fishing offshore in the Gulf of Mexico, we decided to take the crew to lunch. We went to a waterfront restaurant I have been to before. It's a little hard to get to and dock with a larger boat, but the food is always worth it. The food was great as usual, but the service left a little to be desired. When we were greeted, you could tell the server didn't want to be there this day. She didn't ask us how we were and when I asked her how she was, she replied Okay. Since this was not a superlative adjective, one could detect that there was something negative going on in this girl's life. It could have been a fight with a spouse, boyfriend, kids or something else not relevant to our visit. Every request was met by a look that seemed like an inconvenience to her. When you are out on a boat all day, beverage refills are numerous. Hey, we are why you are here. Maybe she was having a bad day or maybe she should have just taken the day off.

If you are waiting tables and can't hide it or fake it, please take the day off or go get a job that requires little or no contact with the public. By the way, the Grouper Sandwiches were excellent!

A large group of us accumulate for dinner as we are at a convention and need food. There were 13 in all and we all decide to go to a Steak and Beer place. There is a short wait for a table and we are in no hurry as everyone is telling war stories. We are seated and greeted and pitchers of beers are ordered. We are a mixed bag of hospitality geeks, males and females, away from home for a few days. It's party time. We order everything on the menu, different steaks, different temperatures and different sides.

This is not a difficult task if you are a professional and know what you are doing. There is a salad bar so that part for the waitress was pretty much a no brainer. The food arrives and the auction began. Who had the????, etc, etc... It really was ok as our spirit was loose and in party mode. The bill arrives and the fun began. We were not on expense report and we are all paying cash so we didn't ask for separate checks. We all know that can be painful, as the key question would be who pays for the pitchers of beer. I handle the bill as I have the highest SAT scores in math and I start the process. I add the beer, divide by 13, add your meal and calculate the tip. This is a simple and now a huge pile of cash has accumulated on the table. This is where it gets interesting.

The waitress overhears my method of calculations and interrupts me to explain I am calculating the tip wrong. She tells me that I should take the total bill and add 20%. This annoys me as I think I've got this covered. I quickly count the pile of cash on the table and we are looking to cover the bill and there is somewhere between 25-30% leftover for her. I am still irked. I decided that management should be aware of how their servers help quests figure out the tip. This is just a professional courtesy, as I thought he should know and my colleuges agree. The manager appears on a timely basis and I explain the situation. I am now shocked at his response. He insisted we leave her nothing; he collected the cash for the bill and bought us two pitchers of beer in the bar and issues a sincere apology. This is a good a manger.

Upon consuming our complimentary beer, I notice a lecture being given to our waitress by my favorite manager somewhere in a discreet location. This advice cost her almost $100. I really hope she didn't lose her job, but I hope she learned an important lesson.

It was a busy day and getting late so we decided to stop for dinner. We stopped at a local Italian restaurant which has a great food reputation. After viewing the menu, everyone was in the mood for pizza. This is an item they do with perfection, served on a stainless steel dessert pedestal. We were greeted by a bubbly attractive waitress and after ordering just a pitcher of Coke and a pizza. I got the look. The look was one of, small bill, small tip and taking up space in my station. The rolling of the eyes always pisses me off. Do that in the kitchen, not in front of me. Her effervescence disappeared. Now that she is stone cold toward us, her anticipation of us leaving could not come soon enough. The bill comes to $20. I paid the bill but I wanted to make a point. On the way out I handed her another twenty dollar bill. I told her the next time she decides to determine what the outcome of the tip will be, think again. I told her, remember this tip.

I have learned over the years that the nicest customers sometimes leave the worst tips. On the other hand some of the biggest buttholes leave the best tips. Keep your game face on all the time and facial expressions should be displayed someplace other than the dining room. I am sure she will always remember that twenty dollar tip.

It's the last day of work for me for a few days as I am embarking on a road trip as my son returns home from college for the summer. I am hoping I will be missed by some who count on my teamwork and conscientious attitude to make the place tick. On the other hand, I will not be missed by the others who think I do nothing all day except when, they figure out, they now have to do what I don't. I am sure I will be talked about, some positive and some negative, as I will be somewhere between 100 and 1200 miles away. I however will not miss any of it. I won't miss the whiners, complainers, the barking Chef, the 10 percenters, and the basic day to day bullshit. I will be enjoying myself, spending time with my son, traveling half way across the country.

There will be no Blogs for a few days as the internet is not available on the road and I will NOT be blogging from my phone. I am sure that I will have some great stories from the six meals I will have on the road and my hotel stay and will catch up upon my return. See Yaaaah!

In a 1200+ mile drive back from Detroit, I saw some interesting but humorous road signs. After passing the Jeep factory in Ohio, I saw two signs, one for the Jeep Parkway and another for Willys Parkway. I was afraid to use them as I was driving an import. I drove through a place called Tipp City. I felt bad because I didn't leave anything. I saw, on the same sign, Sharron Road and Sharronsville. I want to know who Sharon was. In Kentucky, I saw a sign for Boone County. I am sure there is a farm there that makes a really cheap wine. I saw another sign for Buttermilk Pk. I am sure Pk stands for Pancake, not parkway. I started to wonder who picks theses names. I wondered if there were a bunch of good old boys, sitting around, drinking Jack Daniels, with a great sense of humor when they named a park "Big Bone Lick State Park". I also queried about how many car accidents happened on this road before they changed the name to Needmore Rd.

I really shouldn't talk because I live in a town where they name the streets after fruits, pineapple, lime, orange, lemon, etc. When I got home I saw a sign after leaving the airport that said "No Barreling through Work Zones". I love living in a no-nonsense state.

21

Holidays

As we prepare for the upcoming holiday, taking reservations, setting huge buffet tables, Mother's Day is upon us. Hotels will open up their ballrooms, restaurants will come up with special menus, and chefs will work tirelessly to create amazing presentations of gastronomical delights. It is by far the busiest food service day of the year. A little history as in the United States, the holiday dates back to 1908 when Ann Jarvis celebrated it for the first time for her mother. The movement started in the late 1800's to commemorate Mothers who had lost their sons in the Civil War. The holiday was first declared a holiday in West Virginia in 1910 and became an official holiday in 1914. White carnations became a tradition in 1908 as Ann delivered 500 of them to the church service for her mother. It was the favorite flower of her mother. Due to a shortage of white carnations, florists were the catalysts in establishing the tradition of red carnations if your mother was alive and white if your mother was not. She was arrested in 1948 for disturbing the peace by demonstrating because so many people were buying greeting cards instead of writing personal letters. Currently Americans spend $2.6 billion in flowers, $68 million on greeting cards and $1.53 billion on other gifts including jewelry.

We will take Mom to dinner to express our thanks to her for all that she has done. Florist will crank as will all the restaurants and hotels. It is a great holiday. To those of you serving tomorrow, wish all the Moms a Happy Mother's Day, and make a ton of money!!!

Today we celebrate Father's Day but I'm not sure that you know the history behind it. It was a natural event to compliment Mother's Day. Sonora Dodd, whose father was a Civil War veteran, named William Jackson Stuart, was a single parent raising six children on his own. After hearing the sermon at Ann Jarvis' Mother's Day celebration 1909, she felt fathers should have a similar holiday. She spoke to the pastor and wanted to do this on her father's birthday, June 5th. The pastor told he did not have enough time to prepare, so he would do it on the third Sunday of June. Henceforth that's how the traditional date started. So the first father's day was celebrated in 1910 in Spokane Washington. Several attempts were made over the next four decades to make this day a national holiday, but congress thought this was just an attempt to duplicate the commercialization of Mother's Day. Congress continued to defeat these attempts until they were heavily criticized for ignoring one of the two parents. It wasn't until Lyndon B. Johnson issued a Presidential Proclamation honoring fathers in 1966. Six years later, it was made a national holiday by President Richard Nixon in 1972.

I didn't know if you knew how recently Father's Day became a national holiday. Now you have a little trivia to share with your friends. Happy Father's Day to all the fathers out there!!!

Joke was on me. You tell me if you think it was right. I got a call from a co-worker, highly respected co-worker, before today, asking me to come to work to cover for an employee who was still cooked from the previous night. This, not being the first time this has happened, I buy it. A series of necessary protocol phone calls are made and it's confirmed, I am working. It's a Sunday and I am usually off, but with the staff I work with it is common for me to cover some personal disaster on a Sunday. I agree, cancel my plans with a really cute brunette for a seafood festival and head on into work. Upon my arrival, it's an April Fools Prank. Not funny as it's MY DAY OFF! Everyone laughs except me and I depart. This is the Rub. I don't go out much, as I am not into relationships and the luggage it carries with it. It took me three weeks to ask this woman out and she finally agreed. I was kind of pumped up for this. Now I cancel. I am pissed, to say the least, as this is a rare opportunity for me to spend some time with an intelligent being which I don't find in the workplace. At this time I feel like Sissy Spacek in the movie "Carrie" with pig's blood on my head and everyone is laughing at me. Very Funny, but this is at my expense.

I felt like locking all the doors and burning the building down, but Steven King and I aren't on speaking terms right now. I decided to sit on this for a day as most people told me to relax, it was just a joke. I think they went too far. You tell me. I also had to unfriend everyone at work on Facebook the next day. The brunette and I never went out after that.

It's Memorial Day Weekend and it's only the first day and what a day it's been. It starts out a little sluggish and I worked a double yesterday and I am dragging a bit. Early on it looks like everyone is going to make money except me. My station is empty at 8:30am and then boom!! A six top sits in my section and the fun begins. They request separate checks and as I order their food a family of 7 sits next to them. I put in the first order, take the second tables order. Now I deliver the food to the first table and drop the checks. Now it is time to serve the second table. The family is one check, a lifesaver, and I process all the separate checks for the first table. After dropping the family's check, the first table leaves only to be immediately replaced by an 8 top. They order 7 decaf coffees and one regular. I thought for a minute I was in a nursing home. This one is separate checks too. I take their order and send it to the kitchen and then the family pays. After the family leaves the regular Saturday guys show up, requesting me as there server, imagine that. They take up two tables and the fun continues. The eight gets fed, the ten gets fed and everyone pays and I am saying, what an enormous rush. All of this happens in one hour. God I'm good. The rest of the day was a cake walk, comparatively speaking.

Day two of a three day weekend is tomorrow and more than a reasonable amount of sleep is required to make it through the weekend. I am also working an outside catering event tomorrow night (usually followed by an interesting story), after my regular shift and then the celebrated holiday on Monday. Stay hungry my friends and make that money!

22

Summary

 I look at people differently than you do every day. I wonder things like how will they order and how will they tip. I ask myself do they have a great personality or not. Will they be bitchy or friendly? Will they treat me with respect as an equal or talk to me in a way which is demeaning and treat me like a second class citizen because of my occupation.

I will also ponder what people do for a living. I serve for a living and I can always recognize the Hospitality people. I want to visit some of my customers at their jobs and have a little fun. When I arrive there I will deviate from the norm and talk on my cell phone. I will reverse the roles and maybe show less appreciation to you for the services you have provided me with. I want to see the expression on your face when you receive less than you expect.

It is unfortunate that what I do is different than what everyone else does. When you commission my goods and services, you pay after you have consumed them and me. If you don't like what you ordered, it will probably be taken off your check or something new will be made for you. In any other business, you purchase first and then you take it home. If you don't like what you bought, you can take it back or live with it. If you ordered it on-line you know what a hassle it is going to be to return the item. So you probably will just live with it.

When it comes to tipping I really think it should be standardized. It is in Europe and in this country in places like private clubs and all catered events. There are some of you who are not qualified to make the right judgment call regarding what to leave your server. If you order special things, then you will be charged more. Extra is extra. If you require or demand extra services like running us through a bunch of hoops to make you happy, then by the same token you should tip more. Most of you don't.

Serving is an art as well as a profession. If you are dissatisfied with your job as a server you can always find something else to do. It may not be as financially rewarding but it might be less stressful. If you continue to serve for a living then tweak your attitude.

Realize that what you do is just a job. I enjoy mine and you should too. I show up every day and work as hard as I can every day. I make a living out of doing this and hour for hour; it's not a bad living. Lower your expectations. Don't think that everyone is going to tip you 20%. They are not.

Change your mindset to 15% as a goal. You will be happier I promise you. You will be satisfied at the 15%ers and ecstatic at the 20%ers and above. I am sorry however; I cannot do anything about the 10%ers. They will always be like that and maybe when they go to heaven they won't get a window seat, so to speak.

Your work environment will change as well as the people you work with and for. Just accept it. People will come and go. The chef you hate will eventually be replaced with the one you'll love. The asshole manager will move on and someday you will work with more Theory "Y" people than Theory "X" people.

So now that you have adjusted your attitude, go out there and have some fun. Be yourself all the time, be great every day, and go and make some serious money. Bite your tongue every day but smile on the way to the bank.

Good Luck my friends!

www.ingramcontent.com/pod-product-compliance
Lightning Source LLC
Chambersburg PA
CBHW071522180526
45171CB00002B/349